DEMOCRACY IN WHAT STATE?

NEW DIRECTIONS IN CRITICAL THEORY

AMY ALLEN, GENERAL EDITOR

NEW DIRECTIONS IN CRITICAL THEORY

Amy Allen, General Editor

New Directions in Critical Theory presents outstanding classic and contemporary texts in the tradition of critical social theory, broadly construed. The series aims to renew and advance the program of critical social theory, with a particular focus on theorizing contemporary struggles around gender, race, sexuality, class, and globalization and their complex interconnections.

DEMOCRACY

IN WHAT STATE?

Giorgio Agamben

Alain Badiou

Daniel Bensaïd

Wendy Brown

Jean-Luc Nancy

Jacques Rancière

Kristin Ross

Slavoj Žižek

Translations from the French by William McCuaig

COLUMBIA UNIVERSITY PRESS   NEW YORK

COLUMBIA UNIVERSITY PRESS

Publishers Since 1893

New York   Chichester, West Sussex

Library of Congress Cataloging-in-Publication Data

Démocratie, dans quel état?. English

Democracy in what state? / Giorgio Agamben . . . [et al.] ; translations from the
French by William McCuaig.

p. cm.— (New directions in critical theory)

Includes bibliographical references.

ISBN 978-0-231-15298-3 (cloth: alk. paper)— ISBN 978-0-231-15299-0

(pbk : alk. paper) — ISBN 978-0-231-52708-8 (e-book)

1. Democracy—Philosophy.   I. Agamben, Giorgio, 1942–

II. McCuaig, William, 1949–   III. Title.   IV. Series.

JC423.D46313   2010

321.8—dc22

2010023553

CONTENTS

FOREWORD BY THE FRENCH PUBLISHER

Contributors to a number of editions of *La Révolution Surréaliste* in the 1920s were requested to find something new to say about topics on which it seemed at the time that everything sayable had been said— love, suicide, the devil's bargain, things like that. Nevertheless, by casting intersecting beams, the answers they received from Artaud, Crevel, de Naville, Ernst, and Buñuel did succeed in throwing the chosen topics into high relief. This quality of illumination can still surprise us, close to a century later.

The present collection was conceived in homage to that model. The question put to our contributors was this:

The word *democracy* appears to generate universal consensus these days. Of course, debates, sometimes fierce debates, do take place about its meaning or meanings. But in the "world" we inhabit, *democracy* is almost always accorded a positive valence. So we ask our contributors: is it meaningful, as far as you are concerned, to call oneself a democrat? If not, why not? And if so, in line with what interpretation of the word?

Some of the philosophers to whom this question was put were already our collaborators. With others we were acquainted only through writings of theirs, which suggested that their ideas about democracy diverged from the mainstream consensus. The answers you are about to read also diverge from, and sometimes contradict, one another—something we foresaw and counted on. So this book supplies no textbook definition of democracy, nor a user's manual for democrats, and least of all a verdict pro or con. But it does attest that the word *democracy* need not be scrapped just yet, because it still functions as a pivot around which core controversies of politics and political philosophy turn.

TRANSLATOR'S NOTE

I assume responsibility for the English versions of the contributions by Giorgio Agamben, Alain Badiou, Daniel Bensaïd, Jean-Luc Nancy, and Jacques Rancière. The essays by Wendy Brown, Kristin Ross, and Slavoj Žižek were originally composed in English.

Political thought and everyday language in the Anglophone world sometimes ignore the analytical distinction between state and government. The European languages conceptualize the former notion more strongly and capitalize the word (*l'État, lo Stato, el Estado, der Staat*). I deliberately follow this advantageous practice and write "the State" in my translations.

DEMOCRACY IN WHAT STATE?

INTRODUCTORY NOTE ON

THE CONCEPT OF DEMOCRACY

GIORGIO AGAMBEN

The term *democracy* sounds a false note whenever it crops up in debate these days because of a preliminary ambiguity that condemns anyone who uses it to miscommunication. Of what do we speak when we speak of democracy? What is the underlying rationale? An alert observer will soon realize that, whenever she hears the word, it might mean one of two different things: a way of constituting the body politic (in which case we are talking about public law) or a technique of governing (in which case our horizon is that of administrative practice). To put it another way, democracy designates both the form through which power is legitimated and the manner in which it is exercised. Since it is perfectly plain to everyone that the latter meaning prevails in contemporary political discourse, that the word *democracy* is used in most cases to refer to a technique of governing (something not, in itself, particularly reassuring), it is easy to see why those who continue, in good faith, to use it in the former sense may be experiencing a certain malaise. These two areas of conceptuality (the juridico-political and the economic-managerial) have overlapped with one another since the birth of politics, political thought, and democracy in the Greek polis or city-state, which makes it hard to tease them apart. An example will show what I mean. The basic term *politeia* may not be familiar to readers without Greek, but they have seen it translated as *The Republic*, the title of Plato's most famous dialogue. "Republic" does not, however, exhaust its range of meanings. When the word *politeia* occurs in the classical writers, it is usually followed by a discussion of three different forms of *politeia*: monarchy, oligarchy, democracy, or six if you count the three corresponding *parekbaseis*, or deviant forms. But translators sometimes render *politeia* with "constitution," sometimes with "government." In *The Constitution of Athens* (chapter 27), Aristotle characterizes the "demagogy" of Pericles this way: "demotikoteran synebe genesthai ten politeian," and a standard English translation runs "the constitution became still more democratic." Aristotle continues with the statement that "apasan ten politeian mallon agein eis hautous," which the same translator renders as "brought all the government more into their hands." To make his translation coherent, he ought to have written "brought all the constitution more into their hands," but that would obviously have created a difficulty.

When the same fundamental political concept can be translated to mean either "constitution" or "government," then we have ventured out beyond ambiguity onto the featureless terrain of amphibology (a term from grammar and rhetoric signifying indeterminacy of meaning). Let us train our gaze on two further passages from two classics of Western political thought, Aristotle's *Politics* and Rousseau's *The Social Contract*, in which this unclarity manifests itself with particular force. In the *Politics*, Aristole states his intention to itemize and analyze the different "constitutions" or "forms of constitution" (*politeiai*): "Since *politeia* and *politeuma* signify the same thing, and since the *politeuma* is the supreme (*kyrion*) power in a city, it necessarily follows that the supreme power resides either with an individual, with a few, or with the many" (*Politics* 1279a 25 ff.). Current translations run more or less like this: "Since constitution and government signify the same thing, and since government is the supreme power in the state . . ." A more faithful translation would retain the closeness of the terms *politeia* (political activity) and *politeuma* (the resulting political outcome), but, apart from that, it is clear that the essential problem with this passage lies in Aristotle's attempt to get rid of the amphibology by using the term *kyrion*. With a bit of wrenching, the passage can be paraphrased in modern terms as follows: the constituent power (*politeia*) and the constituted power (*politeuma*) bind themselves together into a sovereign (*kyrion*) power, which appears to be that which holds together the two sides of politics. But why is politics riven by this fissure, which the word *kyrion* both dramatizes and heals over?

As for the *Social Contract*, Michel Foucault gave a course in 1977–1978 at the Collège de France showing that Rousseau's aim was precisely to reconcile juridical and constitutional terms like *contract, the general will*, and *sovereignty* with an *art of government*. For our purposes, the important thing is the distinction—basic to Rousseau's political thought—between sovereignty and government and their modes of interaction. In the article on "Political Economy" which the editors of the *Encyclopédie* commissioned from him, Rousseau wrote: "I beg my readers to distinguish clearly between the topic of this article, which is public economy, or what I call government, and supreme authority, or what I call sovereignty. The distinction lies in this: sovereignty has the right to legislate (*le droit legislatif*) . . . whereas government has purely executive power."

In *The Social Contract* the distinction between the general will and legislative capacity, on one hand, and government and executive power, on the other, is restated, but Rousseau now faces the challenge of portraying these two elements as distinct—and yet articulated, knit together, interwoven. This is what compels him, at the very moment he posits the distinction, to deny forcefully that there could exist any division within the sovereign. As with Aristotle, sovereignty, that which is *kyrion* or supreme, is at the same time one of the two terms being distinguished, and the indissoluble link between constitution and government.

Today we behold the overwhelming preponderance of the government and the economy over anything you could call popular sovereignty—an expression by now drained of all meaning. Western democracies are perhaps paying the price for a philosophical heritage they haven't bothered to take a close look at in a long time. To think of government as simple executive power is a mistake and one of the most consequential errors ever made in the history of Western politics. It explains why modern political thought wanders off into empty abstractions like law, the general will, and popular sovereignty while entirely failing to address the central question of government and its articulation, as Rousseau would say, to the sovereign or locus of sovereignty. In a recent book I tried to show that the central mystery of politics is not sovereignty but government; not God but his angels; not the king but his minister; not the law but the police—or rather, the double governmental machine they form and propel.

Our Western political system results from the coupling of two heterogeneous elements, a politico-juridical rationality and an economic-governmental rationality, a "form of constitution" and a "form of government." Incommensurable they may be, but they legitimate and confer mutual consistency on each other. Why does the *politeia* get trapped in this ambiguity? What is it that gives the sovereign, the *kyrion*, the power to ensure and guarantee the legitimacy of their union? What if it were just a fiction, a screen set up to hide the fact that there is a void at the center, that no articulation is possible between these two elements, these two rationalities? What if the task at hand were to disarticulate them and force into the open this "ungovernable" that is simultaneously the source and the vanishing point of any and all politics?

As long as thought balks at tackling this knotty problem and its amphibology, any debate about democracy, either as a form of constitution or as a technique of government, is likely to collapse back into mere chatter.

THE DEMOCRATIC EMBLEM

ALAIN BADIOU

Despite all that is devaluing the word *democracy* day after day and in front of our eyes, there is no doubt that this word remains the dominant emblem of contemporary political society. An emblem is the "untouchable" in a symbolic system, a third rail. You can say what you like about political society, display unprecedented "critical" zeal, denounce the "economic horror," you'll always earn pardon as long as you do so in the name of democracy. The correct tone is something like: "How can a society that claims to be democratic be guilty of this or that?" Ultimately you will be seen to have judged society in the name of its emblem and therefore itself. You haven't gone beyond the pale, you still deserve the appellation of citizen rather than barbarian, you're standing by at your democratically assigned place. Be seeing you at the next election.

Well, I say this: before one can even begin to apprehend the reality of our societies, it's necessary, as a preliminary exercise, to dislodge their emblem. The only way to make truth out of the world we're living in is to dispel the aura of the word *democracy* and assume the burden of not being a democrat and so being heartily disapproved of by "everyone" (*tout le monde*). In the world we're living in, *tout le monde* doesn't make any sense without the emblem, so "everyone" is democratic. It's what you could call the axiom of the emblem.

But our concern is *le monde,* the world that evidently exists, not tout le monde, where the democrats (Western folk, folk of the emblem) hold sway and everyone else is from another world—which, being other, is not a world properly speaking, just a remnant of life, a zone of war, hunger, walls, and delusions. In that "world" or zone, they spend their time packing their bags to get away from the horror or to leave altogether and be with—whom? With the democrats of course, who claim to run the world and have jobs that need doing. What they then find out the hard way is that, warm and cosy in the shelter of their emblem, the democrats don't really want them and have little love for them. Basically, political endogamy obtains: a democrat loves only another democrat. For the others, incomers from zones of famine and killing, the first order of business is papers, borders, detention camps, police surveillance, denial of family reunion. One must be "integrated." Into what? Into democracy, clearly. To be admitted, and perhaps on some distant day greeted, one requires training in democracy at home, long hours of arduous toil before the notion of coming to the real world can even be entertained. Study your integration manual, the good little democrat's handbook, in the intervals between bursts of lead, landings by humanitarian paratroopers, famine, and disease! You've got a stiff exam ahead of you and still no guarantee that you won't find the passage from the false world to the "real" one blocked. Democracy? Sure. But reserved for democrats, you understand. Globalization of the world? Certainly, but only when those outside finally prove they deserve to come inside.

In sum, if the world of the democrats is not the world of everyone, if tout le monde isn't really the whole world after all, then democracy, the emblem and custodian of the walls behind which the democrats seek their petty pleasures, is just a word for a conservative oligarchy whose main (and often bellicose) business is to guard its own territory, as animals do, under the usurped name *world.*

With the emblem dislodged, and the territory seen plainly for what it is—a landscape filled with democrats bustling and reproducing—we can turn to important matters: what conditions must a territory meet before it can present itself speciously as part of tout le monde under the democratic emblem? Or to twist the thought a bit: of what objective space, of what settled collectivity, is democracy the democracy?

At this point we may turn (back) to the moment in philosophy when the democratic emblem was first dislodged: book 8 of Plato's *Republic.* Plato applies the term *demokratia* to a way of organizing the business of the polis, a certain type of constitution. Lenin said the same thing long after: democracy is no more than a particular form of State. But both Plato and Lenin are more interested in the subjective impact of this State form than they are in its objective status. Thought must shift the focus from the legal framework to the emblem or from democracy to the democrat. The capacity of the democratic emblem to do harm lies in the subjective type it molds; and, not to mince words, the crucial traits of the democratic type are egoism and desire for petty enjoyments.

Lin Piao, by the way, was being perfectly Platonic when he said, at the height of the Cultural Revolution, that the essence of false communism (the kind prevailing in Russia) was egoism and that the true motive of the reactionary "democrat" was quite simply fear of death.

Of course, Plato's approach entails a purely reactive part, for he was convinced that democracy would not save the Greek polis, and in fact it didn't. Dare one assert that democracy will not save our beloved West either? Indeed; I daresay it won't, and I would add that this brings us right back to the ancient dilemma: either we reinvent communism or we undergo some reinvented form of fascist barbarity. The Greeks for their part had the Macedonians and then the Romans, and either way it was servitude, not emancipation.

Plato, an aristocrat oriented to the past, reaches for configurations like a philosophically trained military aristocracy, which he imagines to have existed once. In fact, he invents them, aristocratic reactionism generating political myth. There are plenty of contemporary variants of reaction dressed as nostalgia on display. The one most striking to anyone who follows developments here in La République Française is the idolatrous "republicanism" we see pervading our intellectual petite bourgeoisie, where any invocation of "our republican values" is greeted with loud applause. Just remind me again, will you—which republic was it you were referring to? The one created out of the massacre of the communards in 1870? The one that flexed its muscles in colonial conquest? The republic of Clemenceau the strikebreaker? The republic that did such a splendid job of organizing the shambles of 1914–1918? The one that handed plenary power over to Pétain? The hallowed and virtuous "republic" of which you prate has been concocted for the express purpose of safeguarding the democratic emblem, which hasn't been looking too healthy of late. Plato thought he was flying the banner of aristocracy with his philosopher-guardians, but it was tattered and moth-eaten. It's the old story; nostalgia is always nostalgia for something that never existed.

Still, quite apart from its aristocratic reactionism, Plato's critique of democracy retains independent and, indeed, bivalent force. On one hand, it is aimed at the essence, the reality, of the democratic form of State, on the other, at the constitution of the subject—*homo democraticus*—in a world thus formalized. Plato's two theses, which I regard as entirely well-founded and wish to extend a bit beyond the world of the polis, are

1. the democratic world isn't really a world;
2. the only thing that constitutes the democratic subject is pleasure or, more precisely, pleasure-seeking behavior.

In what respect does democracy authorize a pleasure-seeking subject to the exclusion of all else? Plato describes two forms of the relation to pleasure constituted in the democratic nonworld. The first is youthful Dionysiac enthusiasm. The second is elderly indifference to the varieties of pleasure. At bottom, the socialization of the democratic subject begins with the illusion that everything is available. "Untrammeled pleasure!" says the anarchist of '68. "My clothes, my Nikes, and my hash," says the would-be (or perhaps "wannabe") rebel from France's problem suburbs. Yet democratic life comes full circle with the crepuscular awareness of the equivalency, and thus the nullity, of everything except the universal standard of value: money (and the whole apparatus needed to protect it: the police, the justice system, the prisons). From prodigious avidity fancying itself freedom to budgetary avarice with a strong security presence—there you have it in a nutshell.

What has this to do with the world? Any world, for Plato and for me, only becomes visible, is only thrown into relief, by the differences constructed within it, first by the difference between truth and opinion and then by the difference between truths of more than one type (love and politics, for example, or art and science). But within a horizon in which everything is equivalent to everything else, no such thing as a world is discernible, only surfaces, supports, apparitions without number. This is what Plato has in mind when he says that democracy is a form of government "diverting, anarchic, and bizarre, which dispenses an equality of sorts indiscriminately among the equal and the unequal." Diversion is what the young seek, the satisfaction, potential at least, of their wants. What Plato calls the imposition of an artificial equality on things unequal translates seamlessly, for me, into the monetary principle, the universal equivalency or fungibility that bars any possibility of real difference, of the heterogeneous as such (in the way that truth methodically reached is heterogeneous to freedom of opinion). This abased, abstract equality is really no more than a demeaning subjection to quantifiability that interdicts the con-sistence of a world and imposes the rule of what Plato calls "anarchy." Anarchy obtains when value is mechanically attributed to what is without value. A world of universal substitutability is a world without any proper logic of its own, in other words not a world at all, only an "anarchic" whirl of eidola.

What defines the homo democraticus trained into this anarchy is that he or she as subject reflects the substitutability of everything for everything else. So we have the overt circulation of desires, of the objects on which these desires fix, and of the cheap thrills they deliver, and it's within this circulation that the subject is constituted. And as I said, in senescence our subject, blasé by now, comes to accept a certain interexchangeability of those objects, as a boost to circulation (or "modernization"). All he or she can really make out any more are the numbers, the quantities of money in circulation. The pump driving the whole system, though, is the youthful urge to seek pleasure in the satisfaction of desire—from which it follows that, while the *wisdom* of circulation may reside with the old who have come to see that the essence of everything is monetary nullity, its animated *existence*, its incessant self-perpetuation demand that youth occupy the foreground. Homo democraticus is an avaricious old fellow grafted onto a craving adolescent. The adolescent makes the wheels turn, and the old fellow reaps the profits.

Plato lucidly observes the false democratic world in action, compelled to idolize youthfulness while mistrusting youthful enthusiasm. There is something essentially juvenile about the democratic ethos, something that feels like universal puerilization. As Plato puts it, in a false world of that sort "the elderly abase themselves to youthful modes, for fear of seeming tiresome and overbearing." Likewise, in order to collect the dividends of his cynical skepticism, the elderly democrat must pretend to be fighting a youthful battle for more "modernity," more "change," more "rapidity," more "fluidity." It puts one in mind of an aging millionaire rock star, creaking and creased but doggedly bawling into the microphone and thrusting his pelvis this way and that nevertheless.

What becomes of collective life, of the collectivity, when its emblem is eternal youth, when the sense of age has vanished? The answer depends on whether one is observing the state of things in zones where monetary circulation has not yet really shifted into high gear (capitalist gear) or in our zone. Possible outcomes in the former include a sort of terroristic exaltation of the brutality and heedlessness of adolescence. We saw the dreadful consequences of the revolutionary version of this kind of indigent "juvenilism" with the Red Guards of the Cultural Revolution and the Khmer Rouge and the equally dreadful consequences of the deideologized version of the same thing with the terror sown in numerous regions of Africa by armed gangs of adolescents manipulated by outside powers or warlords. Those are limit cases, extreme (but thereby definitive) examples of adolescent democratism unplugged from all the myriad forms of monetary circulation but one, the circulation of lethal firearms in abundance. But what about us? In our zone, the supremacy of youth gives the search for pleasure the force of a social imperative. "Have fun" is the universal maxim. Even those least able to do so are obliged to try to comply. Hence the profound stupidity of contemporary democratic societies.

Plato is a sure and perceptive guide to the panorama of modern society, which is a weave of three main motifs: the absence of world, the democratic emblem as subjectivity enslaved to circulation, and the imperative of universal adolescent pleasure seeking. His thesis is that any society matching that description is on a road to ineluctable disaster, because it is incapable of organizing a discipline of time. Plato puts a famous ironic tribute to the existential anarchy of contented democrats and their "beautiful, youthful, mode of government" in the mouth of Socrates. Here it is, rendered with a certain liberty:

Democratic man lives only for the pure present, transient desire is his only law. Today he regales himself with a four-course dinner and vintage wine, tomorrow he is all about Buddha, ascetic fasting, streams of crystal-clear water, and sustainable development. Monday he tries to get back in shape by pedalling for hours on a stationary bicycle; Tuesday he sleeps all day, then smokes and gorges again in the evening. Wednesday he declares that he is going to read some philosophy, but prefers doing nothing in the end. At Thursday's dinner party he crackles with zeal for politics, fumes indignantly at the next person's opinion, and heatedly denounces the society of consumption and spectacle. That evening he goes to see a Ridley Scott blockbuster about medieval warriors. Back home, he falls to sleep and dreams of liberating oppressed peoples by force of arms. Next morning he goes to work, feeling distinctly seedy, and tries without success to seduce the secretary from the office next door. He's been turning things over and has made up his mind to get into real estate and go for the big money. But now the weekend has arrived, and this economic crisis isn't going away, so next week will be soon enough for all that. There you have a life, or lifestyle, or lifeworld, or whatever you want to call it: no order, no ideas, but nothing too disagreeable or distressing either. It is as free as it is unsignifying, and insignificance isn't too high a price to pay for freedom.[1]

Plato's thesis is that sooner or later this manner of existence, grounded in the indiscipline of time, and its correlative form of State, representative democracy, will bring about a visible manifestation of their despotic essence. Because that is what it comes down to: the real content of all that youth and beauty is the despotism of the death wish. That is why, for Plato, the trajectory that begins with the delights of democracy ends with the nightmare of tyranny. He is proposing that, from a perspective embracing the world and time, there exists a link between democracy and nihilism. For the democratic nonworld is a leakage of time. Consumption is consuming it.

So there it is: the emblem of the modern world is democracy, and youth is the emblem of the emblem, symbolizing as it does the absence of *restraint* on time. Evidently this youth-emblem has no substantial existence. It's an iconic construct generated by democracy, but some constructs are constructive, and this one constructs the bodies it needs out of immediacy (only pleasure-seeking exists), fashion (each present moment substitutable for any other), and stationary movement (*on se bouge,* to use a French idiom).

So not being democratic is the same as getting old or being old? That misses the point entirely. As I said, the old see a lot and absorb a lot. The point is this: if democracy equals monetary abstraction equals an organized death wish, then its opposite is hardly despotism or "totalitarianism." Real opposition is the desire to set collective existence free of the grip of this organization. Negatively, that means the order of circulation must no longer be that of money, nor the order of accumulation that of capital. Private property simply cannot be allowed to dictate how things are going to be. Positively, it means that politics, in the sense of subjective mastery (the mastery of thought and praxis) over the future of humanity will have independent value, obeying its own atemporal norms like science and art. Politics will not be subordinated to power, to the State. It is, it will be, the force in the breast of the assembled and active people driving the State and its laws to extinction.

Plato contemplated these prospects clearly, even if the bounds of his own worldview made him restrict them to the lives of what he called the "guardians" of the city, with everyone else assigned fixed productive tasks. The guardians possess nothing, among them all is communal and shared, and their only power is that of the Idea, for their city has no laws. So let the maxims Plato reserves for his aristocracy of wisdom become the maxims of everyone, of all of us. Antoine Vitez used to say that the theater and art were meant to be "elitist for everybody." Well then, let there be an "aristocratism for everybody." But aristocracy for everybody is just a way of formulating the highest aspiration of communism, and we know that the worker revolutionaries of the nineteenth century saw Plato as the first philosophical spokesman for communism.

You can take any doctrine and label the caricatural reversal of it its opposite, but if you think of its opposite as the moment of its creative fulfillment, when all the excess trappings fall away, then the opposite of the kind of democracy we have had served up to us during the "long good-bye" of capitalist parliamentarism is not totalitarianism or dictatorship. It is communism, which, as Hegel said at the time, absorbs and surmounts the formalism of the age of restricted democracy.

What I have aimed to do here is to set brackets around the authority the word *democracy* is likely to enjoy, or have enjoyed, in the mind of the reader and make the Platonic critique of democracy comprehensible. But, as a coda, we can go right back to the literal meaning of democracy if we like: the power of peoples over their own existence. Politics immanent in the people and the withering away, in open process, of the State. From that perspective, we will only ever be true democrats, integral to the historic life of peoples, when we become communists again. Roads to that future are gradually becoming visible even now.

PERMANENT SCANDAL

DANIEL BENSAÏD

Theater of Shadows

The end of the long wave of post–World War II expansion, the revelations about the extent of the Soviet Gulag, the horror of Cambodia, then the Iranian Revolution and the onset of the neoliberal reaction: there was a shift in world affairs starting around the middle of the 1970s. The protagonists of the cold war—capitalism versus communism, imperialism versus national liberation—faded from the billboards, and a new titanic struggle between democracy and totalitarianism was proclaimed to a drumbeat of publicity. Actually it was more like the restoration of the French monarchy, with the straightforward term *democracy* conferring a threadbare mantle of soft legitimacy on the unfolding of an interminable Thermidor. Yet, then as now, the victorious liberals clung to their secret mistrust of the specter of popular sovereignty lurking beneath the calm surface of democratic formalism. Or not so secret. "I accept the intellectual rationale for democratic institutions," wrote Tocqueville in 1853, "but I am instinctively an aristocrat, in the sense that I contemn and fear the crowd. I dearly love liberty and respect for rights, but not democracy."[1] Fear of the masses and a passion for law and order are the real foundations of liberal ideology. Market despotism and its level playing field manipulate "democratic" discourse the way a ventriloquist manipulates his dummy, making it speak the lines he chooses.

So, in the waning century's theater of shadows, two abstractions, democracy and totalitarianism, were supposed to be slugging it out, while the contradictions at work below the surface of each were repressed.[2] Hannah Arendt, more circumspect, pointed out that "whatever the similarities, the differences are essential." Trotsky may have qualified Hitler and Stalin as "twin stars," and he may have conceived the "statization" (*l'étatisation*) of society as a form of bureaucratic totalitarianism with the motto "La societé, c'est moi."[3] But he never lost sight of the social and historical differences without which no concrete politics is possible.

By one of those ironies with which history is so prodigal, democracy appeared to triumph over its evil twin at the very moment when the conditions that had made it appear that there was an organic link between constitutional freedoms and free enterprise were beginning to unravel. Over three decades of postwar prosperity, the wedding of parliamentary democracy and the "social market economy" under the liberal aegis appeared to promise a future of unlimited progress and prosperity and so to have exorcized at last the specter that had haunted the world persistently since 1848. But, after the crisis of 1973–1974, the postwar tide stopped advancing and began to recede, and that sapped the bases of what was sometimes called the Fordist (or Keynesian) compromise and the social (or "welfare") state.

With the debacle of bureaucratic despotism and "real" (i.e., unreal) socialism, the floating signifier *democracy* became a synonym for the victorious West, the triumphant United States of America, the free market, and the level playing field. Simultaneously a full-scale onslaught against social solidarity and social rights and an unprecedented campaign to privatize everything were causing the public space to shrivel. Hannah Arendt's erstwhile fear of seeing politics itself, meaning conflictual plurality, disappear from the face of the earth, to be replaced by the routine administration of things and beings, was apparently coming about.

The Return of the Good Shepherds

The widely trumpeted victory of democracy soon yielded a crop of new Tocquevilles voicing their ill-concealed dislike of it, reminding their readers that democracy meant more than just unfettered exchange and the free circulation of capital: it was also the expression of a disturbing egalitarian principle. Once again, from the likes of Alain Finkielkraut and Jean-Claude Milner, we heard the elitist discourse of a restricted group worried by the intemperance, excess, and exuberance of the common herd.

Once again we heard vaunting praise of hierarchies of genealogy and the nobility of divine right, as against full citizen equality prevailing over the common space. Once again we heard praise of the measured wisdom of pastoral government, as opposed to the disorder and the "criminal penchant" of democracy. We saw all the upholders of family values, moral values, educational values taking a stand in the name not of democracy but of the positivist Republic and "Progress through Order." Quickly they formed ranks to "dispel their dread that unnameable democracy might be, not a type of society that likes bad government better than good, but the very principle of politics, the principle that gave birth to politics by grounding good government on its own absence of ground."[4]

This holy league of "republican democrats" (*sic*) published an astonishing declaration under the fearful title "Have No Fear!" in *Le*

Monde for September 4, 1998. Good lord, fear of what? Of "action by organized blocs" and "social groups . . . eager to proclaim themselves enraged" so as to prevent the law from being applied. (One wonders: which law exactly?) To exorcize their fear of the social specter, these republican democrats apealed in chorus for "old-fashioned respect." They invoked "deference to breeding, competence, leadership." They expressed nostalgia for the tutelary figures of the "father" and the "lieutenant" (which to French ears connotes stern old-fashioned law enforcement). Their hatred of democracy betrayed giddy fear at the fragile legitimacy of all power and the anguished realization that a challenge to established rights may always be mounted by emergent ones.

Malaise in Market Democracy

The next to voice disquiet after the virtuous republicans were the champions of market democracy. Pierre Rosanvallon diagnosed a democratic malaise, the symptoms of which included "the growing irrelevance of elections . . . the declining centrality of administrative power . . . lack of respect for public officials." The triumph of democracy was just a prelude to its undoing: "Never has there been such a thin line between a positive outlook for democracy and the chance that it might go off the rails."[5] "Menacing swerves" toward antipolitics or depoliticization could only be countered by "an affirmation of the properly political dimension of democracy."

Observing how "society is composed more and more of communities bonded by adversity, kinship, situation, and converging historical trajectories," Rosanvallon insists on the growing importance of compassion and victimhood. From these enumerations social class practically evaporates, as though its dissipation were an irreversible sociological fatality and not the result of political pressure (the ideological and legislative promotion of competitive individualism) on the social realm. Hence the enigma, insoluble in the terms posed by Rosanvallon, of a democracy without quality for humans without qualities: how could a politics without classes be anything but a politics without politics? The narrowed temporal horizon of a present huddled over itself entails the annihilation of politics as strategic rationality, to the sole profit of instrumental and managerial rationality. No surprise, then, that Rosanvallon looks to an enlarged role for appointive as opposed to elective office and a proliferation of "independent authorities" as crutches for the tottering legitimacy of the vote.

The Specter of "Real Democracy"

The indeterminacy of the signifier *democracy* leads to divergent, often opposed, definitions. Raymond Aron's was minimal and pragmatic: democracy is "the organization of peaceful competition to hold the reins of power," in which "political freedom" is a given, for otherwise "the playing field is tilted."[6] There we have it, long before the defunct European constitutional treaty made it famous: the notion of the "level playing field" common to the working of parliamentary democracy and the free market. Who would deny, Claude Lefort chimes in, "that democracy is linked to capitalism while yet distinct from it?" Nobody, of course, the whole problem being to determine in what respects they are historically linked (the advent of territorial citizenship, the secularization of power and law, the shift from divine sovereignty over subjects to the popular sovereignty of the people over the people) and in what respects the former stands apart from, critiques, and surpasses the latter.

The problem was tackled by Marx as early as 1843 in his often misconstrued critique of Hegel's philosophy of law and the State. In his Kreuznach manuscript, "his thought about politics and his thought about democracy appear closely tied."[7] Whereas Tocqueville binds democracy to the State (the "democratic State") the better to detach it from revolution, the young Marx declares that "in real democracy, the political State would disappear." Precociously there emerges the theme of the abolition or withering away of the State. But to claim that in "real democracy" the political State would disappear signifies neither a dissolution of the political into the social nor the hypostasis of the political moment as a form containing the universal: "In democracy none of the moments takes on a meaning that does not belong to it: each is really no more than a moment of the total *demos*." Politics in this perspective is the strategic art of mediation.

Marx's youthful intuitions were more than just caprices, soon to be dropped in favor of a starker vision of the conflictual relation between domination and servitude. "True democracy" is never entirely forgotten. It persists, says Miguel Abensour, as a "latent dimension," the thread linking the youthful texts to the ones on the Paris Commune and the *Critique of the Gotha Program*.

Politics a Rarity, Democracy Intermittent?

The self-contradiction and ambivalence of the democratic pretension have been thrown into strong relief by the pressure of liberal globalization. It's no surprise that the critique of the democratic illusion, and Carl Schmitt's critique of parliamentary impotence, have gained adherents and begun to take revenge on the humanitarian moralism triumphant only yesterday.[8] These radical critiques have a lot in common and may appear to overlap at times. But they aim at different, indeed diametrically opposed, goals.

Alain Badiou's Platonizing critique of "the tyranny of number" and the majoritarian principle leads him to draw a contrast between politics and "the clash without truth of a plurality of opinions." Jacques Rancière draws the contrast differently, between democracy as a permanently expansive movement and democracy the way it is taught in political science departments as an institution or regime. Both appear to share the view that politics is rare and intermittent, belonging to the order of the exceptional event, not that of history and the administration of society. "There is not a lot of it," says Rancière about politics, and it is "always local and occasional." Both offer the same critique of elections as a reduction of the people to statistics. We live in an age of universal assessment, where everything demands to be quantified and measured, where only number has the force of law, where majority is supposed to equal truth, hence these critiques are necessary. But are they sufficient?

Philosopher King

"I have to tell you that I absolutely do not respect universal suffrage for itself alone: it depends on what it does. Why should universal suffrage be the one thing in the world that merits respect independently of its outcomes?"[9] Alain Badiou's challenge to the supremacy of numbers and voting is a salutary reminder that a numerical majority is never proof of truth or justice. But he says nothing about social convention and juridical formalism, without which the law is never more than pure force and pluralism is at the arbitrary mercy of every individual.

Badiou's radical critique relies on identifying democracy with capitalism pure and simple, with the fungibility that makes everything on the market equal in value to everything else.

If democracy is representation, it is representation first and foremost of the general system that bears its forms. In other words, electoral democracy is not representative except to the extent that it is the consensual representation of capitalism, today rebranded "the market economy." Such is its corruption in principle, and one comprehends why Marx thought that, faced with a democracy like that, the only remedy was a transitory dictatorship, which he called the dictatorship of the proletariat. "Dictatorship" is a loaded word, but it does shed light on the chicanery of the dialectic between representation and corruption.[10]

For Marx, though, dictatorship was not in the least the opposite of democracy, and when Lenin spoke of "democratic dictatorship" he didn't mean it as an oxymoron.

Badiou appears to contemplate a chain of discrete historical sequences, each unfolding and reaching its termination independently of the orientations and decisions of the actors, sustained by fidelity to an inaugural event.

The enemy of democracy was not the despotism of a single party (miscalled totalitarianism) except insofar as this despotism brought the first sequence of the communist Idea to an end. The only real question is how to begin a second sequence of this Idea, in which it prevails over the clash of interests by means other than bureaucratic terrorism. A new definition and a new practice, in short, of what was called the "dictatorship" of the proletariat.

In the absence of critical reflection, historical and social, on past sequences, this indeterminate novelty goes nowhere. All it does is refer us to a future experiment. It remains the case, though, that "nothing gets done without discipline," but "the military model of discipline must be surpassed."[11] In the article just quoted, Badiou invokes a third stage of communism, "centered on the end of socialist separations, the repudiation of vindictive egoism, a critique of the motif of identity, and a proposal for nonmilitary discipline." Upon what might this nonmilitary discipline rest? Unknown. Absent agreement democratically arrived at in view of a common project, it can only be the authority of a religious faith or a philosophical doctrine and their word of truth.

Unlike Marx, Badiou does not take a stand at the heart of the effectual contradiction of the democratic theme so as to blow it apart from within. He discards it, pure and simple:

> This point is essential: from the outset, the communist hypothesis coincides not at all with the democratic hypothesis and the modern parliamentarism to which it leads. It subsumes another history, other events. That which appears important and creative in light of the communist hypothesis is different in nature to that which democratic bourgeois historiography chooses to highlight. That is why Marx . . . stands apart from democratic politicking in maintaining, in the school of the Paris Commune, that the bourgeois State, no matter how democratic it might be, deserved destruction.[12]

Yes, but after the destruction? The tabula rasa, the blank page, absolute commencement in the purity of the event? As though the revolution did not weave together event and history, act and process, the continuous and the discontinuous. As though we were not always beginning again in the middle. The question left unanswered by Badiou is that of Stalinism and—though he doesn't confuse them—Maoism. "In Stalin's time," he writes in his anti-Sarkozy pamphlet, "it has to be said that political organizations of workers and people had an infinitely better time of it [in the West], and capitalism was less arrogant. There is no comparison." He meant to be provocative, clearly. If it is indisputable that workers' parties and unions were stronger "in Stalin's time," this bare observation supplies no basis for deciding whether that was *thanks to* or *in spite of* him or, above all, for stating what his policies cost movements of emancipation, then and now. Badiou is more prudent in an interview he gave to *Libération*: "My only tip of the hat to Stalin: he threw a scare into the capitalists."

That's still a tip of the hat too many. Was it Stalin who scared the capitalists, or something else, like the great workers' struggles of the 1930s, the worker militias of Asturias and Cataloña, and demonstrations by the Popular Front—in sum, fear of the masses? In a number of cases, not only did Stalin not frighten the capitalists, he aided them: one thinks of the days of May 1937 in Barcelona, the Hitler-Stalin pact, the big carve-up at Yalta, or the disarming of the Greek resistance.[13]

The critique of Stalinism in Badiou boils down to a question of method: "It is not possible to direct agriculture or industry with military methods, nor to pacify a collective society by State violence. What ought to be indicted is the choice to organize as a party, what one could call the party form." Thus he winds up rehearsing the superficial critique of the disillusioned eurocommunists, who quailed at taking the full measure of the historic transformation that was occurring and chose instead to blame a partisan form and particular method of organization for the disasters of the twentieth century. So it would be sufficient to renounce the "party form"? As though an event as important as a bureaucratic counterrevolution costing millions of dead and deported did not raise questions of a quite different order, questions regarding the social forces at work, worldwide market relations, the effects of the social division of labor, the economic forms of transition, and political institutions. What if the party were not the problem but an element of the solution?

The Irreducible "Democratic Excess"

Ignorant and/or lazy journalists have committed the utter nonsense of likening Jacques Rancière's preference for "democratic excess" to the kind of restricted "participatory democracy" associated in France with Ségolène Royal. The furthest possible thing from a "just order," democracy for him is not a form of State at all. It is "above all this paradoxical condition of politics, the point where all legitimacy confronts its own absence of ultimate legitimacy, confronts the egalitarian contingency that undergirds the inegalitarian contingency itself." It is "action that unceasingly robs oligarchic government of the monopoly of public life, that robs wealth of its omnipotence over lives."[14] It is "neither a form of government nor a mode of social life," but rather "the mode of subjectivation through which political subjects exist" that "aims to dissociate political thought and thought about power."[15] It is not "a political regime," but "the very institution of politics."

During a colloquy at Cerisy, it was put to Rancière that he supplies no practical guidance on strategic questions of organization and party; his reply was that he had "never taken an interest in the organizational forms of political collectives."[16] Distancing himself from speculative leftism, he stresses the importance "of thinking politics primarily as the production of a certain effect," as the "affirmation of a capacity" and the "reconfiguration of the territory of the visible, the thinkable, the possible." In a subsequent interview, though, he adds some nuance: "It is not a question of discrediting the principle of organization and valorizing nothing but explosive scenes. My views stand apart from any polemic or opposition between organization and spontaneity."[17] He aims principally to rethink what politics signifies: "Politics is, in the strict sense, anarchic," by which he means: without primordial foundation.

Withering Away of the State and/or Politics

Agnès Heller and Ferenc Feher experienced the Hungarian revolt of 1956 and bureaucratic despotism in eastern Europe at first hand, so they have solid grounds for their opposition to State fetishism. But they reject "the utopian vision of the total abolition of the State and its institutions." This they regard "not just as an impossible undertaking," but as a utopian one that would hinder the thinking through of "alternative models of the State and institutions, in which alienation would progressively decline." "If the State engrosses society," democratic liberties are condemned to disappear. And "since a society expressing a homogeneous will is inconceivable, we must envisage a system of contracts ensuring that the will and the interests of all are taken into consideration. Hence we must envisage the concrete form that the exercise of democracy will take."[18]

This critique of bureaucratic totalitarianism, as we know, gave the "eurocommunist" parties of the 1980s theoretical justification for surrendering unconditionally to the dictates of ventriloquist capitalism. It does nonetheless highlight the obscurities and perils surrounding Marx's hesitant proposition that the State would or must "wither away." Six weeks of communal liberty in the spring of 1871 were enough to make Marx write that State power was "henceforth abolished." Abolished? That's a bit drastic. It would seem to contradict what Marx had to say in his polemics against Proudhon and Bakunin, in which he opposes the idea that an abolition, of the wage-earning class or the State, could simply be decreed. He sees it as more of a process, the preconditions of which were to be attained through the reduction of hours worked, the transformation of property relations, and the radical modification of the organization of work. Such expressions as the extinction or withering away (of the State) imply a process; like "permanent revolution," they place the emphasis on the link between act and duration.

The withering away of the State should not be interpreted as the absorption of all its functions by social self-management or the simple "administration of things." Certain "central functions" must continue to exist, but as public functions under popular control. Thus the withering away of the State does not signify the withering away of politics or the extinction of it through the simple rational management of society. It can just as well signify the extension of the domain of political struggle through the debureaucratization of institutions and permanent deliberation on public matters. Such an interpretation is confirmed by Engels in 1891: the proletariat, he wrote, cannot keep itself from "gnawing" at the most harmful facets of the State, until "a generation that has grown up in new and free social conditions gains the capacity to do away entirely with the bric-a-brac of the State." It is not a question of abstractly proclaiming the abolition of the State by decree, but of assembling the preconditions allowing it to dispense with its bureaucratic bric-a-brac. The seizure of power is no more than a first step, a beginning, the onset of a process and not its completion.

Rousseau's Fault?

The effective contradictions of democracy (not its "paradoxes,"as Norberto Bobbio once wrote) are inherently present in the aporias (the formal contradictions) of the social contract. From the moment one accepts Rousseau's premise that "might does not make right," and that "one owes obedience only to legitimate powers," the question of the ground of legitimacy arises and with it the insurmountable tension between legality and legitimacy. To appeal to the latter against the former is always an option, and we see the juridical impossibility this leads to in the right to insurrection written into the constitution of Year 11 of the French Revolution.

If liberty is "obedience to self-prescribed law," it entails its own negation, to wit "the total alienation" of each individual member and all his rights to the community, for "in giving oneself over to all, one gives oneself over to no one." Each voluntary associate puts his person "under the supreme direction of the general will," and each becomes "an indivisible part of the whole." Together they constitute a public person or "political body" called the State when it is passive and the Sovereign when it is active. Voluntary submission to impersonal law applying to all replaces the personal dependency and arbitrariness of the ancien régime. But the cost is an exacerbated holism in direct contradiction with the liberal presuppositions of contract and possessive individualism.

This contradiction emerges in the conception of "public possessions" to be set against the unlimited right of private appropriation. If the State is master of all the goods of its members by virtue of the social contract, it follows that every man "naturally has a right to what he requires" and that "the right of each individual to his or her own private property is subordinated to the right the community has over everything." Or, as Hegel puts it, "the right of distress overrides property rights." Hence the social pact institutes moral and legitimate equality between citizens "equal by convention and by right." Rousseau was one of the first with the theoretical intelligence to bind the democratic question to the question of property.

The act of association is "a reciprocal engagement" between the public entity and individuals. It presupposes that each contracting member contracts with himself as a member of the State, a sovereign member, binding himself to a whole of which he is a part. But then the nature of the "political body" entails an impossibility: that the Sovereign could impose on itself a law that it could not itself break. "There cannot be any species of fundamental, obligatory law for the body of the people, not even the social contract." In other words, the contract is always subject to revision, and the constituent power inalienable. From which there logically follows the codification in law of the right to insurrection.

The result is the impossibility of representation, since "the Sovereign, by the fact that he is, is always all that he must be." If sovereignty is simply "the exercise of the general will," it cannot indeed be alienated. Power may be delegated, but not the will. The Sovereign can will "from present moment to present moment" (*actuellement*), but not for the future, for it is absurd that "the will could shackle itself into the future." Here we have the ground of "immediate democracy," where the Sovereign "can never be represented except by himself," which Rosanvallon today rejects.

Improbable Miracle

The general will is of course "always right" and always aims at public utility, but it does not follow that "the deliberations of the people always have the same rectitude": "One never corrupts the people, but one often deceives it." Hence there is no contradiction within the people, but there is deceit, manipulation, propaganda. It's the original version of modern "conspiracy theory," though the modern sort is missing the crucial notion of ideology.[19] It logically follows that, if "the general will can err," it must be because of "prevarication" and "faction," the intrigues of enemies of the people or "partial associations at the expense of the all-embracing association." So, for the general will to manifest itself aright, it is necessary to ban any "partial association" (any party!) in the State, so as to allow "each citizen to speak for himself alone." The formula, emblematic of confidence in the supposedly free and rational subject, converts easily into confidence in the fact that this sum of reasons culminates in Reason. From that to "Reason of State" is but a step.

In Rousseau, however, this confidence is immediately tempered by the idea that while "the general will is always right . . . the judgement that guides it is not always enlightened." He looks for an answer to this troubling observation in pedagogy and education rather than within conflictual experience: when "the public wills the good but does not discern it," it "has need of guides" capable of "showing it the right path" (!).

Hence the general will runs into a democratic deadlock. To set out the best guidelines for social life, "a superior intelligence would be necessary, perceiving all the passions of mankind and feeling none of them," a sort of juridico-moral twin of Laplace's demon. This inaccessible vantage point on totality would make the legislator "in all respects an extraordinary man in the State," for he who commands the laws must not exert command over men. This legislator must resort to a different kind of authority, capable of "inducing without violence and persuading without convincing." To escape from what Hannah Arendt called "the vicious constitutional circle," Rousseau is thus driven to invoke a conventional transcendence—civic religion, which is supposed to bridge the gap between the homogeneity of the ideal people and the divisions among the real people, which he is unable to formulate as a class struggle. And, since "not everyone can make the gods speak," Rousseau plays the joker in the deck, enlightened despotism: "The great soul of the legislator is the real miracle which must prove his mission."[20]

To Think the Institution

Where Rousseau's thought halts, Saint-Just takes over, with his interrogation, on the eve of Thermidor, of the necessity of republican institutions: "The institutions are the guarantee of public liberty, they moralize the government and the civil state" and "ground the reign of justice." For "without institutions, the strength of a republic rests either on the qualities of fragile mortals, or on precarious means."[21] With the guillotine only a few days away, Saint-Just evokes all those who were vanquished in the struggle for emancipation; they "had the unhappiness to be born in countries without institutions; in vain they relied on all the force of heroism; factions, triumphant for a day, cast them down into eternal night, notwithstanding years of virtue." For him, as later for Che Guevara, the "force of heroism" and the virtue of example were not enough to bridge the tragic gap between the constituent power and instituted democracy.

The experience of the "sad truths" of the revolution, wrote Saint-Just in this testamentary document, "made me conceive the idea of shackling crime through institutions." "Institutions have as their object the concrete establishment of all social and individual guarantees so as to avoid dissension and violence, and substitute for the ascendancy of men the ascendancy of morals."[22] It is needful, he insists, as though sending one last message before sinking into the silence of eternal night, "to substitute, through institutions, the strength and inflexible justice of law for personal influence: then the revolution is consummated." Neither he, nor Che Guevara, nor Patrice Lumumba, nor so many others had time to resolve this mysterious democratic equation, the puzzle of which they have handed on to us.

"The social-historical [*le social historique*] is the union of and tension between instituting society and instituted society, between history made and history in the making."[23] To what extent can society be endlessly instituting itself and thus escape the self-perpetuation of the instituted? Such "questions, the question of revolution, do not overleap the boundaries of the theorizable, but instantly locate themselves on another terrain, that of the creativity of history."[24] And I would add: on the terrain of political practice where this creativity is exercised, in a profane history open to the uncertainty of struggle.

The Stress of Uncertainty

Claude Lefort terms democracy a "form of society in which men consent to live under the stress of uncertainty" and "where political activity runs up against its limit." By definition, it is exposed to the paradox of the skeptical relativist who doubts everything except his own doubt, to the point of becoming a dogmatic doubter, a doctrinaire of doubt. Conscious of this danger, Lefort admits that "relativism attains its highest degree when the point is reached where the value of democracy is queried."[25] How to escape this uncertainty, inscribed as it is in the very principle of democratic equality?

The answer would be to "laicize democracy," to pursue the transformation of theological questions into profane ones and so cease trying to reduce the political to the social, searching for a mythical lost unity. Such a pretension that the social might absorb the political completely, that a mythical "great society," a primordial *Gemeinschaft*, might be regained, presupposes a homogeneous society that contrasts with the irreducible heterogeneity of the social. The experience of totalitarian regimes, Lefort states, teaches us the impossibility of imagining "a point of fulfillment of the social, where all relations would be seeable and sayable."

From a stance almost diametrically opposed, Rancière also considers "the ideal reduction of the political by the social" as the sociological termination of the political, as a reduction of democracy to "the political self-regulation of the social." In the 1970s "pure politics" and its ideologues returned in force, though this was presented as a revival of "political philosophy." For Rancière this was a way of hiding the fact that "the social is not a proper sphere of existence, but a litigious object of the political." There is a political (and imaginary or symbolic) institution of the social. And "the debate between the philosophers of the return of the political and the sociologists of its termination" was no more than a phoney debate "about the order in which the presuppositions of political philosophy should be taken so as to interpret the consensual practice of the annihilation of the political."

Secularizing Democracy?

Not to personify society, not to believe that it might act as a "body"— these were the pragmatic concerns of Walter Lippmann in the interwar years, when he saw the political space being destroyed by the negation of class conflict in the interests of a popular State or "State of the entire people." "Society does not exist" he was finally provoked to say. For him, as for John Dewey, to laicize democracy was to reject any notion of the beyond, any transcendence, any next world, any ultimate foundation, and to accept the insurmountable uncertainty of political judgment. Dewey addressed himself to Trotsky on this point. For Trotsky, utilitarian morality, the justification of the means by the ends, was anathema; his focus was on the justification of the ends themselves, but ultimately the criterion he invoked was the class struggle. Dewey accused Trotsky of thus surreptitiously resorting to a factitious transcendence. There is no escape from the circle of interaction between ends and means, and political decisions always contain an irreducible element of uncertainty. We cannot not be involved, we have to place our bets.

Lippmann opposed mystical conceptions of society that would "prevent democracy from attaining a clear idea of its own limits and the goals it might actually reach."[26] Its business is to resolve, prosaically and without a universal moral code, simple conflicts of interest. Lippmann cherished no illusion that some sort of correct popular will might be expressed through the ballot box, since voters have no time to "examine problems from all sides." Some had hazarded the notion that, since politics is not a profession, the sum of individual incompetences could still make democracy collectively competent. Lippmann answered with skeptical lucidity that "there is not the slightest reason to think, as mystical democrats do, that the sum of individual ignorances could produce a continuous force capable of directing public affairs." Since nobody can take an interest in all the issues, the ideal outcome would be for those directly involved in a dispute to reach agreement, the experience of "one who is party to a cause" being fundamentally different to the experience of someone who is not.

For Lippmann the inevitable conclusion was that the democratic ideal could never, on account of excessive ambition, lead to anything but disappointment and a drift toward forms of invasive tyranny. So it was necessary to "put the public in its place" in both senses: remind it of its obligation to behave modestly and give it a seat in the grandstand, as a spectator.[27]

Discordant Space and Time

For Rancière, representation is "fully and overtly an oligarchic form." Right from the start it is "the exact opposite of democracy."[28] For Cornelius Castoriadis, as for Lefort, "the disincorporation of power" implies, on the contrary, a "scene of representation." Representative democracy is more than just the system in which the representatives participate in political authority in the stead of the citizens who have chosen them, imparting "relative visibility" to society at the price of sometimes quite severe distorsions. Above all, it provides a designated space for controversy so that the common interest can prevail over corporatism. He sees its dynamic principle as "full recognition of social conflict, and of the differentiation of the political, economic, juridical, and aesthetic spheres, of the heterogeneity of morals and behavior."[29]

Hence representation is seen as the consequence not just of society's irreducible heterogeneity but also the unharmonized plurality of social spaces and times that grounds plurality and the necessary autonomy of social movements vis-à-vis both the parties and the State. Functioning like a gearbox, coupling discordant temporalities, or a mobile ladder connecting unarticulated spaces, the political struggle determines their always provisional unity, from the vantage point of totality.

Hence the extension of individual liberties becomes indissociable from the advent of a public space. When this public space withers, political representation becomes farce and buffoonery. During the interwar years it turned into what Hannah Arendt called an "operetta." Or a tragic comedy.

Direct or Corporatist Democracy?

Short of imagining the temporal and spatial conditions for direct democracy in the strict sense (without mediation) in which the people themselves are permanently assembled, or a system of drawing lots in which the designated individual performs a function without having any mandate conferred on him or representing anyone, delegation and representation are inevitable. It is true in a city, true during a strike, true in a party. Rather than try to deny the problem, it would be better to tackle it head on and search for the modes of representation guaranteeing the closest control of their mandatories by the mandators and limiting the professionalization of the exercise of power.

The 1921 debate between Lenin and the worker opposition is informative in this respect. Aleksandra Kollontay accused the party leadership of adapting to "heterogeneous aspirations," of seeking input from specialists, of professionalizing power, of resorting to "peremptory control, the incarnation of an individualistic conception characteristic of the bourgeoisie." She was perceptive enough to see, before others, the professional dangers of power and discern the nascent bureaucratic reaction taking shape. But her criticism, which was that these deviations were the result of concessions to the heterogeneity of society, presupposes the phantasm of a homogeneous society: with the privileges of property and birth abolished, the proletariat would be one body. Who is meant to ensure the creativity of the dictatorship of the proletariat in the economic domain, Kollontay asked: "The essentially proletarian organs which are the unions" or "on the contrary, the State administration, which lacks a living relationship with productive activity and, moreover, is *of mixed social background?*" "The core of the problem lies there," she added.[30]

There the core does indeed lie. The upshot of doing away with territorially based representation (the soviets were originally territorial bodies)[31] was a tendency to transform the unions into administrative or statist organs and to hamper the emergence of a general will by maintaining corporatist fragmentation. From the pen of Kollontay, as from that of her partner Chliapnikov, there flowed denunciations of "variegation" and "mixed social composition." They were denouncing concessions made to the petite bourgeoisie and the managerial class of the old regime ("these *heterogeneous categories* among which our party is obliged to tack and trim"). This phobia about mixture and motleyness is revealing of a dream of a sociologically pure workers' revolution without hegemonic intent. Its paradoxical outcome was the single party, the incarnation of a single, unified class.

What Lenin was combating back then, in the guise of the worker opposition, was in reality a corporatist conception of socialist democracy, juxtaposing without melding the particular interests of localities, enterprises, and trade, while failing to isolate a general interest. It thus became inevitable that this network of decentralized powers and local economic democracy, which was incapable of proposing a hegemonic project for the whole of society, should be crowned by bureaucratic Bonapartism. The controversy bore not on the validity of the partial experiences inscribed in the real movement aiming to abolish the existing order but on their limitations.

On the Relativity of Number

Number has nothing to do with truth. It never has the force of proof. Majority rule can, by convention, bring debate to an end, but the avenue of appeal always remains open: against today's majority from today's minority, from the present to the future, from legality to legitimacy, from law to morality.

The radical alternative to the majoritarian principle, the drawing of lots, is no more than a "least-bad" option. It is not surprising that the idea should be bruited about once again, if only in mythical form, as a symptom of the crisis of our current democratic institutions.[32] Rancière supplies the most serious argument for it. "The deepest trouble conveyed by the word democracy," he writes, is the absence of any title to govern. Democracy "is at the mercy of the god of chance," it is the scandal of a superiority grounded in no other principle than the absence of superiority. Hence the drawing of lots is the logical conclusion. It has its drawbacks, no doubt, but all in all it is less detrimental than government by competence, collusion, and intrigue: "Good government is the government of equals who do not wish to govern." As for democracy, it is "neither a society for governing, nor a government of society, it is properly this ungovernable thing upon which all government must, in the last analysis, discover that it is grounded."[33] The straightforward substitution of sortition for representation would thus signify not only the abolition of the State, but of politics in the sense of deliberation out of which may arise proposals and projects to be accomplished.

Contrary to a tradition that preferred to see majorities as immanent manifestations of divine wisdom, Lippmann for his part defends a desacralized and minimalist conception of the vote. Casting a vote is not even the expression of an opinion, just a simple promise to support a given candidate. In line with the idea that the voter is competent only regarding that which concerns him personally, Lippman radicalizes the principle of delegation to the point of theoretically accepting the extreme professionalization—and monopolization—of political power. In other words, a de facto return to an oligarchic conception.

Partisan Mediation

Rancière sees fatigue as the force "compelling people to accept being represented by a party."[34] The blanket rejection of representation entails the categorical rejection of the very notion of party: political parties are manifestations of a refusal to exist on one's own. In 1975 Claude Lefort saw parties as the very embodiment of corporatism. Unlike Castoriadis, at that time he rejected, out of principle, any manifesto or program tending toward an all-embracing vision. In 1993, having demonstrated, through unwavering support for NATO's war in the Balkans and Israel's occupation of the Palestinian territories, his commitment to the scenario of frontal opposition between totalitarianism and democracy, he opined that, however pertinent it might be, criticism of political parties should not "cause us to forget the constitutive need of liberal democracy for a representative system." While attributing an indispensable role to civil society's network of associations, he was now prepared to posit that "only competition among political parties brings out the general aspects of the aspirations of various social groups."[35] By an irony of history, he thus found his tortuous way back to the Leninist idea that, the political being irreducible to the social, it is determined in the last analysis by class relations operating through the party struggle.

As for Pierre Bourdieu, in his late years his rejection of democratic faith in the correctness of the mathematical sum of individual opinions lead him to logically reemphasize the importance of collective action, no matter what name was given to this collectivity. But a party is not a class, and class is never containable within parties that claim to represent it. So there is "an antinomy inherent in politics": the risk of plunging into alienation through delegation and representation, under the pretext of escaping alienation in the workplace. Because the dominated do not exist as a group (except statistically) prior to the operation of representation, they require representation somehow or other. This leads to an almost perfect vicious circle of domination and "the fundamental, virtually metaphysical, question of what it means to speak for people who would have no voice at all if one did not speak for them."[36]

A metaphysical question, indeed, or a false problem. It follows ineluctably from the tenacious prejudice to the effect that the dominated are incapable of breaking out of the vicious circle of represen-tation and speaking for themselves. Yet the dominated do speak up—and dream—in any number of ways. Contrary to what Bourdieu asserts, they exist in many modes, including the group mode, prior to the "operation of representation," and the countless words of work-ers, women, and slaves bear witness to this existence. The specific problem is that of their political speech. As Lenin demonstrated, po-litical speech is not a faithful reflection of the social, nor a code into which corporatist interests are translated. It has its own displace-ments and symbolic condensations, its specific sites and speakers.

The Theological Annihilation of Political Parties

Today rejection of the "party form" generally goes along with a strong preference for ad hoc coalitions and fluid, networklike, intermittent and affinity-based forms. Such discourse is not all that new, being isomorphic to liberal rhetoric about free circulation and the liquid society. In her *Note on the General Suppression of Political Parties*,[37] Simone Weil was not content to adopt a pose of self-sufficient "partyless-ness." She was prepared to suggest "starting to get rid of political parties." This notion flowed logically from her diagnosis that "the structure of every political party" entails "a prohibitive anomaly": "a political party is a machine for fabricating collective passion, for ex-erting collective pressure on everyone's thinking." Hence every party is "totalitarian in origin and inspiration."[38]

She was expressing, from the standpoint of a revolutionary syndi-calist, the same criticism of political parties we hear today. After the lived experience of the Spanish Civil War, the Hitler-Stalin pact, and the Stalinist "big lie," she had her reasons: the horror she felt at the evolution of the great party machines of the interwar years and the stifling of political pluralism. Along with that went a strongly expressed preference for "not joining up" (naively seen as a token of individual freedom) and "an unconditional desire for truth." The latter is self-evidently linked to a religious conception of truth revealed by grace: "Truth is one." "Only the good is an end." But who proclaims this absolute truth and who decides on this sovereign good?

Abandon politics and one is left with theology: "The inner light always gives a manifest answer to whoever consults it." But "how to desire truth without knowing anything about it?" That, admits Simone Weil, is "the mystery of mysteries," the elucidation of which is purely tautological. Truth arises from the desire for truth: "Truth is the thoughts that rise up in the mind of the thinking creature uniquely, totally, exclusively desirous of truth. It is in desiring truth without preconceptions, and without attempting in advance to guess its content, that one receives the light." Such a revelation through grace, such a quest for purity, lead inevitably to the paradox of authoritarian individualism: *à chacun sa vérité*. Rejecting any collective authority, it ends by arbitrarily imposing its own authority. So for Weil "the suppression of political parties would be a virtually unalloyed good."[39] Indeed? What would take their place? Weil imagines an electoral system in which the candidates, rather than proposing a program, would limit themselves to profferring a purely subjective opinion: "I think this or that about this major issue or that one." So no more parties, no more left or right, just a dust cloud of shifting opinions: those elected would associate and disassociate in accordance with "the way things naturally played out, and the movement of affinities." To keep these fluid and intermittent affinities from crystallizing or coagulating, it would be necessary to go to the extreme of forbidding occasional readers of a magazine from organizing themselves into a society or group of friends: "Every time a milieu attempted to harden into a group by establishing definite criteria for membership, criminal charges would be laid once the fact was established" (!).[40] Which leads to the question of who promulgates the law and in whose name such criminal proceedings would be launched.

The refusal of profane politics, with its impurities, uncertainties, and wobbly conventions, leads ineluctably back to theology and its jumble of graces, miracles, revelations, repentances, and pardons. Illusory flights from the sordidness of politics actually perpetuate impotence. Instead of pretending to wriggle out of the contradiction between unconditional principles and the conditionality of practical living, politics means taking a stand there and working to surmount it without ever suppressing it. Get rid of mediation by political parties and you will have the single party—even the single State—of the "partyless." There is simply no way out.

Mistrust of the partisan mindset is legitimate. But it is an overreach to impute to a form, the "party form," exclusive responsibility for the threat of bureaucracy and the ills of the century. The strong tilt toward bureaucratization is inherent in the complexity of modern societies and the logic of the social division of labor. It haunts all forms of organization. The suppression of political parties that Simone Weil calls for amounts to reverse fetishism, a flat organizational determinism that naturalizes the organization instead of historicizing it, instead of thinking through its evolutions and variations as a function of changes in social relations and the media of communication.

Permanent Democratic Revolution

Contrary to what is widely believed, Marx was not voicing contempt for democratic freedoms when he characterized them as "formal." A jurist by training, he knew well enough that forms are not vacuous and have an efficacity of their own. But he did lay emphasis on their historic limits: "Political emancipation [recognition of civil rights] is a great advance; it is certainly not the ultimate form of human emancipation in general, but it is the last form of human emancipation in the order of the world as we have known it to date."[41] For him the task was to replace "the question of the relation between political emancipation and religion" with that of "the relation of political emancipation to human emancipation," of political democracy to social democracy. The task of revolutionizing democracy, which became practical with the revolution of 1848, remains to be accomplished, if criticism of parliamentary democracy as it really exists is not to slide toward authoritarian solutions and mythic communities.

Rancière speaks of the "democratic scandal." Why does he choose to call democracy scandalous? Precisely because, to survive, it must keep pushing further, permanently transgress its instituted forms, unsettle the horizon of the universal, test equality against liberty. Because democracy incessantly smudges the uncertain divide between the political and the social and stoutly challenges the assaults of private property and the infringements of the State on the public space and public goods. It must ultimately attempt to extend, permanently and in every domain, access to equality and citizenship. So democracy is not itself unless it is scandalous right to the end.

"WE ARE ALL DEMOCRATS NOW . . . "

WENDY BROWN

"Welcome Back, Democracy!"
—Headline, article on Obama election, *The Beaver*
(London School of Economics newspaper),
November 6, 2008

Democracy as Empty Signifier

Democracy has historically unparalleled global popularity today yet has never been more conceptually footloose or substantively hollow. Perhaps democracy's current popularity depends on the openness and even vacuity of its meaning and practice—like Barack Obama, it is an empty signifier to which any and all can attach their dreams and hopes. Or perhaps capitalism, modern democracy's nonidentical birth twin and always the more robust and wily of the two, has finally reduced democracy to a "brand," a late modern twist on commodity fetishism that wholly severs a product's salable image from its content.[1] Or perhaps, in the joke on Whiggish history wherein the twenty-first century features godheads warring with an intensity that ought to have been vanquished by modernity, democracy has emerged as a new world religion—not a specific form of political power and culture but an altar before which the West and its admirers worship and through which divine purpose Western imperial crusades are shaped and legitimated.

Democracy is exalted not only across the globe today but across the political spectrum. Along with post–cold war regime changers, former Soviet subjects still reveling in entrepreneurial bliss, avatars of neoliberalism, and never-say-die liberals, the Euro-Atlantic Left is also mesmerized by the brand. We hail democracy to redress Marx's abandonment of the political after his turn from Hegelian thematics (or we say that radical democracy was what was meant by communism all along), we seek to capture democracy for yet-untried purposes and ethoi, we write of "democracy to come," "democracy of the uncounted," "democratizing sovereignty," "democracy workshops," "pluralizing democracy," and more. Berlusconi and Bush, Derrida and Balibar, Italian communists and Hamas—we are all democrats now. But what is left of democracy?

Rule by the Demos

It cannot be said often enough: liberal democracy, Euro-Atlantic modernity's dominant form, is only one variant of the sharing of political power connoted by the venerable Greek term. *Demos + cracy = rule of the people* and contrasts with aristocracy, oligarchy, tyranny, and also with a condition of being colonized or occupied. But no compelling argument can be made that democracy inherently entails representation, constitutions, deliberation, participation, free markets, rights, universality, or even equality. The term carries a simple and purely political claim that the people rule themselves, that the whole rather than a part or an Other is politically sovereign. In this regard, democracy is an unfinished principle—it specifies neither *what* powers must be shared among us for the people's rule to be practiced, *how* this rule is to be organized, nor by *which* institutions or supplemental conditions it is enabled or secured, features of democracy Western political thought has been haggling over since the beginning. Put another way, even as theorists from Aristotle, Rousseau, Tocqueville, and Marx through Rawls and Wolin argue (differently) that democracy requires the maintenance of precise conditions, rich supplements, and artful balances, the term itself does not stipulate them. Perhaps this is another reason why contemporary enthusiasm for democracy can so easily eschew the extent to which its object has been voided of content.

De-democratization

If it is hard to know with certainty why democracy is so popular today, it is easier to adumbrate the processes reducing even liberal democracy (parliamentary, bourgeois, or constitutional democracy) to a shell of its former self. How has it come to pass that the people are not, in any sense, ruling in common for the common in parts of the globe that have long traveled under the sign of democracy? What constellation of late modern forces and phenomena have eviscerated the substance of even democracy's limited modern form?

First, if corporate power has long abraded the promise and practices of popular political rule, that process has now reached an unprecedented pitch.[2] It is not simply a matter of corporate wealth buying (or being) politicians and overtly contouring domestic and foreign policy, nor of a corporatized media that makes a mockery of informed publics or accountable power. More than intersecting, major democracies today feature a merging of corporate and state power: extensively outsourced state functions ranging from schools to prisons to militaries; investment bankers and corporate CEOs as ministers and cabinet secretaries; states as nongoverning owners of incomprehensibly large portions of finance capital; and, above all, state power unapologetically harnessed to the project of capital accumulation via tax, environmental, energy, labor, social, fiscal, and monetary policy as well as an endless stream of direct supports and bailouts for all sectors of capital. The populace, the demos, cannot fathom or follow most of these developments let alone contest them or counter them with other aims. Powerless to say no to capital's needs, they mostly watch passively as their own are abandoned.

Second, even democracy's most important if superficial icon, "free" elections, have become circuses of marketing and management, from spectacles of fund-raising to spectacles of targeted voter "mobilization." As citizens are wooed by sophisticated campaign marketing strategies that place voting on a par with choosing brands of electronics, political life is increasingly reduced to media and marketing success. It is not only candidates who are packaged by public relations experts more familiar with brand promulgation and handling the corporate media than democratic principles; so also are political policies and agendas sold as consumer rather than public goods. Little wonder that the growing ranks of CEOs in government is paralleled by the swelling of academic political science departments with faculty recruits from business schools and economics.

Third, neoliberalism as a *political rationality* has launched a frontal assault on the fundaments of liberal democracy, displacing its basic principles of constitutionalism, legal equality, political and civil liberty, political autonomy, and universal inclusion with market criteria of cost/benefit ratios, efficiency, profitability, and efficacy.[3] It is through a neoliberal rationality that rights, information access, and other constitutional protections as well as governmental openness, accountability, and proceduralism are easily circumvented or set aside and, above all, that the state is forthrightly reconfigured from an embodiment of popular rule to an operation of business management.[4] Neoliberal rationality renders every human being and institution, including the constitutional state, on the model of the firm and hence supplants democratic principles with entrepreneurial ones in the political sphere. In addition to dethroning the demos in democracy, this transformation permits expanded executive state powers at the very moment of declining state sovereignty, about which more in a moment. Having reduced the political substance of democracy to rubble, neoliberalism then snatches the term for its own purposes, with the consequence that "market democracy"— once a term of derision for right-wing governance by unregulated capital—is now an ordinary descriptor for a form that has precisely nothing to do with the people ruling themselves.

But capital and neoliberal rationality are not the only forces responsible for gutting liberal democratic institutions, principles, and practices. Rather, fourth, along with expanded executive power, recent decades have witnessed the expanded power and reach of courts—domestic as well as international.[5] A variety of political struggles and issues, including those emerging from domestic social movements and international human rights campaigns, are increasingly conferred to courts, where legal experts juggle and finesse political decisions in a language so complex and arcane as to be incomprehensible to any but lawyers specializing in the field. At the same time, courts themselves have shifted from deciding what is prohibited to saying what must be done—in short, from a limiting function to a legislative one that effectively usurps the classic task of democratic politics.[6] If living by the rule of law is an important pillar of most genres of democracy, governance by courts constitutes democracy's subversion. Such governance inverts the crucial subordination of adjudication to legislation on which popular sovereignty depends and overtly empowers and politicizes a nonrepresentative institution.

Fifth, along with the domination of politics by capital, the overtaking of democratic rationality with neoliberal rationality, and the juridification of politics, globalization's erosion of nation-state sovereignty as well as the detachment of sovereign power from nation-states is also crucial to the de-democratization in the West today.[7] If nation-state sovereignty was always something of a fiction in its aspiration to absolute supremacy, completeness, settled jurisdiction, monopolies of violence, and perpetuity over time, the fiction was a potent one and has suffused the internal and external relations of nation-states since its consecration by the 1648 Peace of Westphalia. However, over the past half century, the monopoly of these combined attributes by nation-states has been severely compromised by ever-growing transnational flows of capital, people, ideas, resources, commodities, violence, and political and religious fealty. These flows both tear at the borders they cross and crystalize as powers within, thus compromising nation-state sovereignty from its edges and its interior.

When states remain fiercely agentic amidst their eroding sovereignty, when they detach from the unique double meaning of sovereignty in democracies—popular and supervenient—there are two especially important consequences. On the one hand, democracy loses a necessary political form and container and, on the other, states abandon all pretense of embodying popular sovereignty and hence carrying out the will of the people, a process already inaugurated by the neoliberal governmentalization of the state already mentioned. With regard to the first, democracy, rule by the people, is only meaningful and exercisable in a discreet and bounded entity—this is what sovereignty signals in the equation of popular sovereignty with democracy. Democracy detached from a bounded sovereign jurisdiction (whether virtual or literal) is politically meaningless: for the people to rule themselves, there must be an identifiable collective entity within which their power sharing is organized and upon which it is exercised. Of course, the vastness of the nation-state already limits the kinds of power sharing that makes democracy meaningful, but when even this venue gives way to postnational and transnational fields of political, economic, and social power, democracy becomes incoherent.

With regard to the second, states detached from sovereignty become rogue states in both their internal and external dealings. The reference point for ordinary exercises of state power is neither representation nor protection of the people (the latter being the classic liberal justification for state prerogative power). Rather, faintly echoing the raison d'état of the old realists, contemporary states substitute for pursuit of the prestige of power a complex double role as actors within, facilitators of, and stabilizers for economic globalization. In this context, the people are reduced to passive stockholders in governmentalized states operating as firms within and as weak managers of a global order of capital without, an order that has partly taken over the mantle of sovereignty from states. Nothing made this more glaringly apparent than state responses to the finance capital meltdown in the fall of 2008.

Finally, securitization constitutes another important quarter of de-democratizing state action by Western states in a late modern and globalized world. The ensemble of state actions aimed at preventing and deflecting terrorism in Israel and India, Britain and the United States are often mischaracterized as resurgent state sovereignty, but, like state bailouts of capital, are actually signs of the detachment of state from sovereign power and have everything to do with this loss of sovereignty. Facilitated by neoliberal displacements of liberal political principles (liberty, equality, the rule of law) for an emphasis on costs, benefits, and efficacy, the security state reacts to eroding and contested state sovereignty with a range of inadvertently de-democratizing policies, from suspended rights of movement and information access to racial profiling to increased zones of state secrecy and permanent undeclared wars.

In sum, for the people to rule themselves, they must be a people and they must have access to the powers they would democratize. Globalization's erosion of nation-state sovereignty undermines the former and neoliberalism's unleashing of the power of capital as an unchecked world power eliminates the latter. But, if "actually existing democracy" is in a woeful state, let us consider what, if anything, remains of democracy's raison d'être.

Democratic Paradoxes

As is well known, ancient Athenian democracy excluded 80–90 percent of the adult Attican population from its ranks—women, slaves, free foreign residents, and others who did not meet the strict lineage requirements for citizens. These exclusions of Western democracy in its cradle were extreme, but not the exception. Democracy as concept and practice has always been limned by a non-democratic periphery and unincorporated substrate that at once materially sustains the democracy and against which it defines itself. Historically, all democracies have featured an occluded inside—whether slaves, natives, women, the poor, particular races, ethnicities, or religions, or (today) illegals and foreign residents. And there is also always a constitutive outside defining democracies—the "barbarians" first so named by the ancients and iterated in other ways ever after, from communism to democracies' own colonies. In our time, the figure of "Islamicism" comforts democrats that they are such, even and perhaps especially in the face of de-democratization in the West. Thus has an overt antiuniversalism always rested at the heart of democracy, suggesting that if the imperial dream of universalizing democracy materialized, it would not take the shape of democracy.

If premodern, republican democracy was premised on the value of ruling in common—rule by the common for the common—and hence centered on a principle of equality, the promise of *modern* democracy has always been freedom. Modern democracy has never pledged equality except in the most formal sense of representation (one person—one vote) or equal treatment before the law (not a necessary entailment of democracy, rarely secured in practice, and irrelevant to substantive equality). Rather, it is Rousseau's difficult wager—that we surrender ungoverned individual liberty for collective political power, and this in order to realize our individual freedom—that lies at the heart of the normative supremacy claimed by democracy. Indeed, individual freedom remains democracy's strongest metonymic associate today even while its promise of rule by the people is often forgotten.[8] Only democracy can make us free because only in democracy do we author the powers that govern us.

In modernity, freedom understood as self-legislation is presumed a universal human desire, if not, as Kant, Rousseau, and Mill had it, the quintessence of being human. Indeed, it is modernity's birth of the a priori free moral subject that establishes democracy as the only legitimate modern Western political form. This is the figure of the subject that made and continues to make democracy's legitimacy literally incontestable. At the same time, the white, masculine, and colonial face of this subject has permitted and perpetuated democracy's hierarchies, exclusions, and subordinating violences across the entirety of its modern existence. Thus does an overt and perhaps even necessary unfreedom rest at the heart of democracy, suggesting that if the imperial dream of freeing all people was to materialize it would not take the shape of democracy.

The Impossibility of Freedom

Modern democracy's normative presumption is self-legislation attained through shared rule of the polity; the sovereignty of the subject is linked to the sovereignty of the polity, each securing the other. But legislation of what, rule of what? Theorization of a range of normative (formally nonpolitical) powers combined with devastating critiques of the Kantian subject have together rendered freedom especially complex and elusive in late modernity. What powers must we govern, what must we legislate together, what forces must we bend to our will to be able to say we are even modestly self-governing or self-legislating? Answers to these questions have divided democrats across the ages. At one end, liberals make elected representation for lawmaking the core of the matter, along with sharp limits on the transgress of individual activities and ends. At the other end, Marxists insist that the means of existence must be collectively owned and controlled as a first condition of human freedom. Radical democrats emphasize direct political participation while libertarians would minimize political power and institutions.

Once we surrender the conceit of the a priori moral subject for an appreciation of the panoply of social powers and discourses constructing and conducting us, it is impossible to be sanguine about the liberal formulation. Popular assent to laws and representatives is insufficient to fulfill democracy's promise of self-legislation. Instead, we would have to seek knowledge and control of the multiple forces that construct us as subjects, produce the norms through which we conceive reality and deliberate about the good, and present the choices we face when voting or even legislating. Power understood as making the world and not simply dominating it—or, better, domination understood as fabrication and not only rule or repression of the subject—requires that democrats reach deep into polyvalent orders as powers for the grounds of freedom. The simple idea that we and the social world are relentlessly constructed by powers beyond our ken and control immolates the liberal notion of self-legislation achieved through voting and consent. And yet the notion of democratically ruling all the powers constructing us is absurd: it approximates pulling ourselves up by our own bootstraps or grasping from without the psyches through which we experience and know the world. So democracy, to be meaningful, must reach further into the fabrics of power than it ever has and, to be honest, must give up freedom as its prize. From this angle, democracy could never be achieved but is only an (unreachable) aim, a continuous political project; democratization commits its signatories to sharing in the powers that make, order, and govern them, but is perpetually unfinished.[9]

As troubling to the liberal formulation as the Foucauldian- and Derridean-inspired concerns with forms of power other than law and command is the force of capital in making and arranging democratic subjects, already discussed. What can democratic rule mean if the economy is unharnessed by the political yet dominates it? Yet what could be more of a fantasy than the notion of subordinating a global capitalist economy and its shaping of social, political, cultural and ecological life to democratic political rule or, for that matter, to any political rule?

In sum, apart from state power, both capital and a range of less forthrightly economic normative powers must be reckoned with when considering prospects for redemocratization today. History features no success, or even sustained experiments, with democratizing either. So continued belief in political democracy as the realization of human freedom depends upon literally averting our glance from powers immune to democratization, powers that also give the lie to the autonomy and primacy of the political upon which so much of the history and present of democratic theory has depended.[10] Alternatively, this belief entails thinking and practicing democracy with a realist's acute attention to powers democracy has never before tried to theorize, address, or subdue.[11] For the second possibility, a sharper break with liberalism's monopoly on the term *democracy* is hard to imagine.

Do Humans Want Freedom? Do We Want Humans to Be Free?

There is one last contemporary challenge for those who believe in popular rule, perhaps the most serious challenge of all. As we have already said, the presumption of democracy as a good rests on the presumption that human beings want to be self-legislating and that rule by the demos checks the dangers of unaccountable and concentrated political power . But, today, what historical evidence or philosophical precept permits us to assert that human beings want, as

Dostoyevsky had it, "freedom rather than bread?" All the indications of the past century are that, between the seductions of the market, the norms of disciplinary power, and the insecurities generated by an increasingly unbounded and disorderly human geography, the majority of Westerners have come to prefer moralizing, consuming, conforming, luxuriating, fighting, simply being told what to be, think, and do over the task of authoring their own lives. This was the conundrum for the future of liberation first articulated by Herbert Marcuse in the middle of the last century.[12] And if humans do not want the responsibility of freedom, and are neither educated for nor encouraged in the project of political freedom, what does this mean for political arrangements that assume this desire and orientation? What extreme vulnerability to manipulation by the powerful, along with domination by social and economic powers, does this condition yield? Plato worried that improperly ordered souls in charge of their own political existence would author decadence and unchecked licentiousness, but there is a more evident and worrisome danger today: fascism authored by the people. When nondemocrats are housed in shells of democracies, clutched with anxiety and fear in an increasingly unhorizoned and overwhelming global landscape, and ignorant of the workings of the powers that buffet them, how can they be expected to vote for, let alone more actively pursue, their own substantive freedom or equality, let alone that of others?

On one side, then, we face the problem of peoples who do not aspire to democratic freedom and, on the other, of democracies we do not want—"free" peoples who bring to power theocracies, empires, terror or hate-filled regimes of ethnic cleansing, gated communities, citizenship stratified by ethnicity or immigration status, aggressively neoliberal postnational constellations, or technocracies promising to fix social ills by circumventing democratic processes and institutions. Contouring both possibilities is the problem of peoples oriented toward short-run gratifications rather than an enduring planet, toward counterfeit security rather than peace, and disinclined to sacrifice either their pleasures or their hatreds for collective thriving.

Rousseau so deeply appreciated the difficulty of getting a corrupted people oriented toward public life that his commitment to democracy is often seen to have impaled itself on the project of converting such a people into democrats. There are many ways of understanding what he meant by "forcing someone to be free" but all converge on suspending the commitment to freeing the subject in order to realize that commitment. Today, however, it is hard to imagine what could compel humans to the task of ruling themselves or successfully contesting the powers by which they are dominated.

Possibilities

Does the poor fit of popular rule with the contemporary age add up to a brief for abandoning left struggles for democracy and soliciting left creativity in developing new political forms? Or does it, instead, demand sober appreciation of democracy as an important ideal, always unavailable to materialization? Ought we to affirm that democracy (like freedom, equality, peace, and contentment) has never been realizable, yet served (and could still serve?) as a crucial counter to an otherwise wholly dark view of collective human possibility? Or perhaps democracy, like liberation, could only ever materialize as protest and, especially today, ought to be formally demoted from a form of governance to a politics of resistance.

I am genuinely uncertain here. What I am sure of, however, is that this is not a time for sloganeering that averts our glance from the powers destroying conditions for democracy. Encomiums from left philosophers and activists to "deepen democracy," "democratize democracy," "take back democracy" "pluralize democracy" or invest ourselves in a "democracy to come . . . " will only be helpful to the extent that they reckon directly with these powers. We require honest and deep deliberation about what constitutes minimal thresholds of democratic power sharing, whether and why we still believe in democracy, whether it is a viable form for the twenty-first century, and whether there are any nonchilling alternatives that might be more effective in holding back the dark. Is there some way the people could have access to the powers that must be modestly shared for us to be modestly self-legislating today? Is the freedom promised by democracy something humans want or could be taught to want again? Is this freedom likely to yield the good for the world? What kind of containment or boundaries does democracy require, and, if these are not available, is democracy still possible? If we were able to arrive at answers to these questions, there still remains the most difficult one: how the demos itself could identify and reach for the powers to be handled in common if democracy is to become anything more than a gloss of legitimacy for its inversion.

FINITE AND INFINITE DEMOCRACY

JEAN-LUC NANCY

I

Is it at all meaningful to call oneself a "democrat"? Manifestly, one may and should answer both "no, it's quite meaningless, since it is no longer possible to call oneself anything else," and "yes, of course, given that equality, justice, and liberty are under threat from plutocracies, technocracies, and mafiocracies wherever we look." *Democracy* has become an exemplary case of the loss of the power to signify: representing both supreme political virtue and the only means of achieving the common good, it grew so fraught that it was no longer capable of generating any problematic or serving any heuristic purpose. All that goes on now is marginal debate about the differences between various democratic systems and sensibilities. In short, *democracy* means everything—politics, ethics, law, civilization—and nothing.

This loss of significance we ought to be taking seriously, and we are, as the "inquest" the reader is holding in her hand demonstrates. The task for thought is to stop letting common sense pullulate with free-floating incoherencies the way it does now and force democratic nonsignificance to stand trial in the court of reason.

I resort to this Kantian metaphor because I do actually think that we are under pressure similar to that which drove Kant to undertake a critical probe of exactly what it was that "knowledge" meant. To summarize Kant's problem drastically, the distinction between knowledge of an object for a subject and knowledge of "a subject without object" could simply not be ignored any longer. Today it is incumbent on us to become, over time, capable of a demarcation just as clear and consistent between two different meanings, values, and outcomes jumbled together in the nonsignifying word *democracy*.

If I may prolong the Kantian analogy, one mode of this word designates something like what he calls "understanding." Democracy means the conditions under which government and organization are de facto possible in the absence of any transcendent regulating principle (assuming for present purposes that neither "mankind" nor *le droit* [law, right] has transcendental value).

In another mode resembling Kantian "reason," democracy designates the Ideas of Mankind and/or World, inasmuch as they postulate their own capacity to be subjects of unlimited transcendence and complete autonomy despite having renounced their belief in worlds beyond this one and regarding their own immanence and individuality as sacrosanct. (Readers will detect the Kantian undertone even in the use of the verb *postulate* to designate the legitimate mode of an opening to the infinite under the regime of finitude, of "God is dead.")

This second acceptation won't be found in any dictionary and certainly can't be called the "proper meaning" of democracy. But that is the meaning that clings to it, nevertheless: democracy promotes and promises the liberty of the whole human being within the equality of all human beings. In this sense, modern democracy does engage, absolutely and ontologically, the human being and not just the "citizen." Or, rather, it tends to merge the two. In any case, modern democracy corresponds to much more than just another political mutation. We are talking here about a mutation of culture and civilization so profound that it attains the same anthropological proportions as the technological and economic mutations that have come along with it. That's why Rousseau's contract doesn't just institute a body politic: it produces mankind *itself*, the humanity of mankind.

2

For a single word to turn into an amphibology like that, some sort of ambiguity or confusion or unclarity must have prevailed on the register where it originated and came into use. In this case, the register was *politics,* and out of the constitutive duality or duplicity of that word there flows the ill-discerned and ill-regulated ambivalence of the word *democracy.* Over the whole span from the Greeks to us, politics has implied the mere regulation of common existence, on one hand, and some sort of heavenly assumption into the meaning or truth of this existence, on the other. One moment politics is clearly demarcating its own sphere of action where it claims authority, the next it is pushing to take charge of the totality of existence, individual and collective. Not surprisingly, it was the moment of heavenly assumption that presided, like an astrological sign, over the great attempts at political accomplishment of the twentieth century. Not surprisingly, we saw the mere administration of relations and forces surpassed and (self-) sublimated into common being (*l'etre commun*), and whatever this moment of self-sublimation called itself ("the people," "the community," or even "*la république*"), it was an exact reflection of the thrust at the heart of politics to surpass itself, even if that means the notion of a separate sphere labeled "the political" vanishes and the State is absorbed or dissolved. It is out of this thrust toward self-surpassing and self-sublimation that the ambivalence and nonsignificance of the word *democracy* follow.

3

So there we have it: *politics* itself is where it all arises. For politics did arise, after all. We often lazily assume that there is and always has been politics everywhere. No doubt there has always been power everywhere. But there hasn't always been politics. Along with philosophy, it is a Greek invention, and like philosophy it is an invention arising out of the declining presence of the numinous (of agrarian cults, for example), out of the decline of theocracy. *Mythos* gives way to *logos*; the god-king recedes and the order of politics commences.

Prior to anything else, democracy is theocracy's "other." That makes it the "other" of law dispensed from on high as well. Law is something it has to invent while inventing itself. We tend, for understandable reasons, to paint Athenian democracy in rosy hues. But, if you study its history, you see that right from the outset there was an uneasiness. The feeling that it constantly needed to be reinventing itself never went away. The whole affair of Socrates and Plato, the search for a logocracy that could rectify the shortcomings of democracy, unfolds against that backdrop. It's a search that has basically been going on ever since, and there have been many transformations. The most important was the attempt to put public law on a staunchly autonomous footing, with the emergence of the State and State sovereignty.

By transferring sovereignty to the people, modern democracy forced out into the open something that the mirage of monarchical "divine right" (the French variant at any rate) had barely kept veiled anyway: the fact that sovereignty is grounded neither in *logos* nor in *mythos*. From birth, democracy, Rousseau's democracy, knew itself to be without foundation. That was a blessing and a defect at the same time—an anomaly never felt more keenly than we feel it today.

Our task now is to try to figure out where the blessing and the defect may respectively be leading us.

4

We may start by observing that, right from its first iteration, democracy has always been accompanied by a "civic religion." To put it another way: for as long as democracy enjoyed self-confidence, it was aware that it needed to neutralize theocracy—not by "secularizing" it, of course, but by inventing a functional equivalent (not a surrogate) of law dispensed from on high, a figure of donation to cast its aegis over the invention that was coming into being. Democracy required a religion that, without grounding law, would bless its political creation.

So Athens and Rome had their political religions. But these seldom or never possessed all the tutelary power expected of them, and they were subject to wear: it was not a random circumstance that Socrates was condemned for impiety toward the Athenian civic religion, or that Christianity split off from both Jewish theocracy and the Roman civic religion (the latter already weakened through loss of faith in the republic). Philosophy and Christianity are both implicated in the long decline of civic religion in antiquity. Christianity was more than just another theocracy or civic religion. The conjunction of throne and altar in Christianity was always ambivalent, an affair of association and dissociation, partition and competition. New forms of civic religion were either direct offshoots of Christianity (in America) or imitations of it (in France), but they were always bound to be more civic than religious and, in any case, as long as we are discussing words and their meanings, more political than spiritual.

We focus far too little on Plato's relation to democracy, because we revere the man who may not have been the first philosopher in the strict chronological sense, but who was, in effect, the founder of philosophy. But the mismatch between our reverence for him and our democratic *habitus* causes us to see his hostility toward the Athenian regime, which he knew at first hand, as a simple quirk, an aristocratic mindset. Much more is at stake however: Plato blames democracy for not being grounded in truth and therefore illegitimate from the very beginning. Suspicion toward the gods of the polis, and suspicion toward gods and myths in general, opens up the prospect of a foundation of the polis in *logos* (or, what amounts to the same thing, in *theos* in the singular).

5

From then on, our history has two alternatives: either politics (with law) is ungrounded and should stay that way or else it seeks to endow itself with a ground or foundation, a "sufficient reason" à la Leibniz. In the first case, for lack of reason(s), it contents itself with motives like security, mutual interest, and protection against nature and unsociability. In the second case, the reason or Reason invoked (divine right or reason of State, national or international myth) unfailingly turns the shared heavenly assumption it proclaims into domination and oppression.

The fate of the notion of "revolution" was played out in the tension between these two alternatives. Democracy comes right out and demands a *revolution*: a shift in the very basis of politics, frank acceptance of the absence of foundation. But a complete revolution, a 360-degree revolution, would bring the situation back to the supposed point of foundation. Democracy interrupts that; it suspends the revolution.

In recent years, various thinkers have offered us their take on the suspended revolution, on the insurrectional moment as opposed to the hardening into place of the revolutionary State, on politics as an ever-renewed act of revolt, critique, and subversion stripped bare of foundational pretense, on the option of continual harassment rather than overthrow of the State. (The word *State* means literally that which is established, guaranteed, and thus supposedly grounded in truth.) These ideas have merit: they throw into relief the fact that "politics" is not the same thing as the heavenly assumption either of humanity or the world (since by now mankind, nature, and the universe are indissociable). They are a necessary step toward the dissipation of what will prove to have been one of modernity's grand illusions, the illusion that generates a longing for the State to disappear altogether, for a foundation acknowledged as nonexistent to be replaced by a foundation in truth. And where does truth reside? In the democratic apotheosis of mankind (and the world) into a realm of equality, justice, fraternity, and freedom from power of any kind.

It is necessary now to take a further step, to start thinking about how politics without foundation, politics in a State of permanent revolution (if that expression can stand) must permit spheres that are, strictly speaking, foreign to it, to expand on their own. The spheres I mean are those of truth and meaning, the ones labeled more or less correctly *art, thought, love, desire,* and all the other possible ways of designating rapport with the infinite—or, to put it better, of infinite rapport.

To think the manner in which these spheres are heterogeneous to the properly political sphere is a *political* necessity. But what we have got into the habit of calling democracy, tends, on the contrary, to present these spheres or orders as homogeneous. Even if it remains vague and confused, this supposed homogeneity misleads us.

6

Before continuing, let us pause for a moment of linguistic reflection. Maybe it's because the etymological process is intrinsically meaningful, maybe it's a historical accident (the two are hard to tell apart when it comes to the formation and evolution of languages), but either way the current state of our political lexicon supplies food for thought. *Democracy* is a combination of two root words, the second of which (*-cracy*) refers to force and violent imposition, unlike the root *-archy*, which relates to power that is grounded, legitimated by some principle. The point will be clear in reviewing the distinction between two sets, the first comprising plutocracy, aristocracy, theocracy, technocracy, autocracy, even bureaucracy (or for, that matter, ochlocracy, the power of the mob) and the second comprising monarchy, anarchy, hierarchy, oligarchy. A precise analysis of the history of all these terms (and a host of other interesting ones that come to mind, like nomarchy, tetrarchy, physiocracy, mediocracy), entailing proper consideration of how languages differ by epoch, social level, and register, would take us too far afield. But, broadly speaking, readers will have no trouble seeing that there is a distinction between what the termination *-cracy* implies, which is domination by force, and what the termination *-archy* implies, which is a principle of foundation, of ground, of groundedness. There are a few interesting corollaries: one observes that whoever coined the word *theocracy* was implicitly critiquing the legitimacy of direct divine sovereignty, and that *aristocracy* may likewise be thought to allude implicitly to a contradiction between the idea that some people are "the best" and the reality of power exercised arbitrarily by elites.

But that's enough linguistics. The point is that the word *democracy* seems to contain an internal barrier to the possibility of a foundational principle. Indeed, I would go so far as to say that democracy essentially implies an element of *anarchy*. You might even call it principled anarchy, if that adjective and noun could stand to be coupled.

There is no "demarchy," no principle of foundation in "the people," only the oxymoron or paradox of a principle lacking a principate. That is why the *right* or *law* the democratic institution generates has no real existence other than its own unceasing and active relationship to its own lack of foundation. And why the early modern period coined the expression "natural law/right" and why the philosophical implications of this expression continue to rumble somewhere in the background when we hear allusions to "human rights," or those of animals or children or foetuses or the environment, or even nature itself.

There is something we really should get straight once and for all, since its theoretical basis and consequences are well known: not only is there no such thing as "human nature," but "humankind" (*l'homme*) is virtually incommensurable with anything you could call a "nature" (an autonomous and self-finalized order), because the only characteristics it has are those of a subject without a "nature" or one that far outstrips anything we could call "natural"—in a certain sense (either pernicious or felicitous depending on one's point of view) the subject of a *denaturation*.

Democracy, as a species to the genus politics, is incapable of being grounded in a transcendent principle. So the only thing that grounds or founds democracy is an absence: the absence of any human nature.

7

What does this entail on the plane of political activity and institutions? We may examine the consequences in terms of *power* and *society*.

Democracy has a problem with power, because the kind of idiosyncratic *right* or *law* (*droit*) that democracy generates appears to imply or does imply (appearance and reality being precisely the point at issue) a disappearance or trend toward the disappearance of any specific, separate instance of power. As we have seen, though, it is precisely when that line gets blurred that problems arise. Maybe there would be no need for a separate instance of power among some godlike race of men gathered in permanent assembly, with delegates recallable at any time being dispatched to attend to various tasks. It was the ideal behind what, in the history of political thought, is known as the "councils" model or *soviet* model. But although varieties of comanagement or participation deriving from this model may be possible and desirable on a small or intermediate scale, it is simply not practical for society as a whole.

But this isn't just an effect of scale. Something essential is at stake. *Society* exists inasmuch as there exists *exteriority* in relationships. From this perspective, "society" only starts where *interiority* stops, where in-group bonding through kinship and totemic figures or myths ceases. One might even posit that the distinction or opposition, implicit in all the thinking of the classic age about mankind's "unsocial sociability" (Kant) and explicitly available since the end of the nineteenth century, between "society" and "community" is organically linked to democracy. The dissolution of rural community life is organically linked to the rise of cities in the same way. To cross from the rural community into the polis or into the modern megacity is already a step from interiority to exteriority. Exteriority was the problem, or problematic (if that Gallicism can stand), that democracy was called upon to resolve.

I take the liberty of using the terms *interiority* and *exteriority* a bit loosely here, as a species of shorthand, but they are useful heuristics for certain aspects of modern society (another loose term, but well enough understood) I wish to isolate. Modern society exists as, self-represents as, the exteriorized interrelationship of members (individuals) motivated by interest and power. A whole anthropology is silently conjured up the moment one mentions "society" or sociality, or sociability, or association. These words evoke a whole *métaphysique* (another Gallic idiom). To associate is to act in exteriority, and in exteriority it is likewise possible to end the association at will, to dissociate. The interiority/exteriority distinction also illuminates why it is that in society the only aspect power wears is that of "legitimate violence." In interiority it wears myriad other aspects depending on symbolic functions linked to the "internal" truths of myriad groups.

To resume then: the problem democracy has with power is its innate reluctance to use or wield power of the "exterior" kind, the kind that, when used, makes starkly evident the absence of the kind of symbolism of which feudal allegiance and national unity and all religions, civic or not, were and are such potent bearers. From this perspective, the true, longed-for name of democracy, the name that it did in fact engender and that was its horizon for 150 years, was communism. Whether that dreaded word belongs entirely in and to the past is something I don't intend to go into here. But I do interpret *communism*, again from this perspective, as an expression of society's drive to be more than a society—to be a *community* with a symbolic truth of its own. That was the idea behind the word, if you can even call it an idea; it certainly wasn't a concept in the strict sense, more of an urge or impulse of thought impelling democracy to interrogate its own essence and ultimate purpose.

Simply to denounce this or that "betrayal" of the communist ideal is a very inadequate response today. What I would stress is this: there was no onus on the communist idea to be an ideal (utopian or rational), since it was never meant to function as the dialectical relay between social exteriority and common or communitarian interiority (or symbolicity or ontological consistency). But it was meant to raise the problem that *society*, as such, can't and doesn't either raise or face: the symbolic or ontological dimension, or, more bluntly, the meaning and truth, of being-together as a group or community.

Communism's horizon was not the horizon of what we call "the political." It rejected the separation between the political and what I called the other spheres of truth and meaning, but that rejection was not itself political. Communism never understood this; it is our job to understand it now.

But for that, in the circumstances in which we now find ourselves, it is important not to deceive ourselves about power. Power isn't just an expedient for external use, a partly effective bridle on unsociable humanity forced into association. Power isn't just the lust-object of appetites utterly external, indeed, coldly foreign or outright hostile, to the social body. For this "body" is precisely what is at issue: is society a body at all, with organic interiority, or is it just an aggregate, susceptible, at most, to organization?

The fact that power organizes, manages, and governs—that in itself is not a reason to condemn its demarcation into a separate sphere. Hence, no matter how "communist" we may wish we were, we are today having to reckon with the necessity, the need, for the State. Problems like international law and the limits of classical sovereignty are concomitants of the need for the State, not objections to it.

This is not a call for us to resign ourselves to the inevitable. There is more to power than just a basic imperative of government. Power is a kind of desire, an impulse to dominate and a corresponding impulse to submit. We cannot reduce all the phenomena (political, symbolic, cultural, intellectual, verbal, or visual) of power to the mechanistic play of forces incompatible with morality or with the ideal of a just and fraternal community. Yet disapproval of that kind always taints our analysis of power and its forms. This is reductive and ignores the difference between the power impulse and the mere urge to wreak death and destruction. The power impulse is certainly the drive for mastery, for sway, for domination; the drive to seize command and govern. But that is only part of the spectrum or panorama. Along with the furious drive to cast others into subjection, to render them contemptible, to wreak destruction, we are perfectly entitled (whatever psychoanalysis may say) to contemplate the other side of the coin: the ardor of assuming control, the capacity to constrain, contain, and shape, with a view to a form and all that a form may yield. It is not possible to avoid the conjunction and intermixture of these two aspects, and no use wishing for an "impulse police" to tell the difference between the bad dominations and the good domestications. Barbarism and civilization are in dangerous proximity to one another here, but this danger is a sign that the drive for power, for mastery and possession, is indeterminate and, so to speak, open or open-ended.

It is a life drive and a death drive, the drive of a subject in expansion and an object in subjection. It is the waxing of being in desire and the waning of being in satisfaction and fulfillment. It is what Spinoza meant by *conatus* and Nietzsche by *the will to power* and what many other philosophers have perceived and analyzed as well—never without ambivalence, given that the power drive has no predetermined goal or purpose.

Of course political power is meant to protect social life, even to the extent of challenging and altering its inherited arrangements. But that's the point. Power is in place to enable societized human beings to work out their own goals for themselves, goals over which power as such is powerless: the endless ends of meaning (*les fins sans fin du sens*), of meanings, of forms, of intensities of desire. The power drive outstrips or surpasses power, while at the same time seeking power for its own sake. The surpassing of power is the very principle of democracy—but as its truth and grandeur (indeed its majesty), not as its annihilation.

8

These truths about power are no mystery to anyone. After all, it has always been taken for granted, except under mindless tyrannies, that the governors govern for the good of the governed. (As a corollary, one might even posit that, in all cases except those of pure tyranny, the people are the ultimate font of power whether the regime is expressly democratic or not.) But "the good of the governed" is just a check on the exercise of power, not a determination of the nature, form, or content of what it is that is *good* for them.

Essentially, this good is not determined (which doesn't mean indeterminate) and can only determine itself in the movement that invents or creates it, without ever dispelling interrogation—disquiet, *élan*—about what it may be or become. The forms and meanings, the fundamental stakes, of every existence are unknown at the outset (and, for that matter, we set out again and again). All that we can know boils down to two propositions: our existence is without any prior design, destiny, or project; and it is neither individual nor collective, since existence, the truth of "being," is something that only comes about within the plurality of individuals into which dissolves any postulate of the unity of "being."

The good without project or unity lies in the ever-recurrent invention of forms through which meaning comes about. *Meaning* means: sending from some to others, circulation, exchange or sharing of possibilities of experience, in other words, of relation to the external, relation to the possibility of an opening onto the infinite. Commonality (*le commun*) is the whole point here. Meaning, meanings, sensation, sentiment, sensibility, sensuality only occur (come about, are given) in commonality. More exactly, they are the very condition of commonality: mutuality of feelings, hence exteriority neither converted into or fulfilled in interiority, but tensed, set in tension, among us.

To the extent that democracy entails a *métaphysique* (or, if one prefers, ends or goals to which it might relate) which it is unable to guarantee through religion, civic or not, democratic politics must make it plain that the play of meaning and meanings lies beyond its control. This has nothing to do with public versus private or the collectivity versus the individual. It is a question of *commonality* or the *in-common* (*l'en-commun*), which is neither one nor the other and consists only in being neither. *Commonality* is the regime of the *world*, of the circulation of meanings.

The sphere of the common is not unique: it comprises multiple approaches to the order of meaning—each of them itself multiple, as in the diversity of the arts, thought, desire, the affects, and so on. What "democracy" signifies here is the admission—without any heavenly assumption—of all these diversities to a "community," which does not unify them, but, on the contrary, deploys their multiplicity, and with it the infinite of which they constitute the numberless and unfinalizable forms.

9

The trap that politics set for itself with the birth of modern democracy—meaning once again democracy without any effective principle of civic religion—is what generates confusion between the enforcement of social stability (the State in the etymological sense, *lo Stato*, the stable State) and the idea of a form incorporating all the expressive forms of being-in-common (that is, of being or existence tout court, absolutely).

It is not that it is illegitimate or vain to aspire to a form of all forms. In one sense, each form strives toward that, whether it be through one of the arts, or through love, thought, or knowledge. But each knows, and knows with an innate, originary knowledge, that its own aspiration to envelop and sweep up all forms declares its truth only when it opens itself to their multiple developments and allows inexhaustible diversity to proliferate. Our drive for unity or synthesis knows itself, when it knows itself aright, as a drive for expansion and unfurling, not contraction into an end point. The gravitational pull of the end point and the unique meaning distorts the understanding of politics.

Look at things in the perspective of line and desire, resonance and language, calculation and gesture, cuisine or drapery: there is no regime of form that doesn't, in the end, expand by working on all the others, through contact or sending, through contrast or analogy, along paths direct, or circuitous, or broken, yet none thereby intends to absorb or unify the others. That would be self-negation. If "the brass awakes as bugle" ("le cuivre s'éveille clairon," Rimbaud), that's because it wasn't its lot to be a violin.

Neither is there a form of forms, nor is totality ever achieved. On the contrary, the *total* (*le tout*) keeps pressing for more (even emptiness or silence), because it would explode if it didn't. Yet "politics" allowed it to be thought that something like totality might be attainable and, for that "political" reason, was driven to erase its own boundary by claiming that "everything is political" or that politics takes precedence over any other praxis.

Politics must give the form of access to openness of the other forms: it is the antecedent of a condition of access, not of a foundation or determination of meaning. That does not subordinate politics, but it does confer upon it the particularity of supreme service. It must ceaselessly renew the possibility of the unfurling of the forms or registers of meaning. In return, it must not constitute itself as form—or not in the same sense at any rate: the other forms and registers do in effect envelop ends that are ends in themselves (the arts, language, love, thought, knowledge . . .). But, in compensation, it allows the imposition of form on power to take place.

Politics never attains ends. It leads to plateaus of transient equilibrium. Art, love, and thought are entitled every time, at every occurrence, so to speak, to proclaim themselves accomplished. But, at the same time, these fulfillments are only valid in their proper spheres, and have no claim to make either law or politics. Thus one might posit that these registers belong to the order of a "finishing off of the infinite," whereas politics pertains to indefinition.

10

I will stop, not conclude, with a few discrete remarks.

The delimitation of the nonpolitical spheres (the ones I called art, love, thought, and so on) is neither given nor immutable; the invention of these spheres, their formation, their transformation into figures and rhythms—for example, the modern invention of "art"—itself belongs to this regime of invention of ends and their transformation, reinvention, and so on.

Neither is the demarcation that separates the political sphere from all the others given or immutable. Example: where should a "cultural politics" start or stop? Democracy is what it is because it has to reflect on its own internal demarcation of the political sphere.

What I have said might be taken to legitimate the actual state of things in our democracies as they are. Politics does indeed observe lines of partition with the spheres denominated *artistic, scientific, amorous*—yet never stops intervening, in a hundred different ways, in each of them. But what is never stated or thought through is precisely what I am trying to force into visibility: that politics *is not* the locus of the heavenly assumption of ends, only the locus of access to their possibility. To invent the locus, the organ, the discourse that would make it possible to think this through would be a notable political feat.

Democracy is the appellation of a mutation in humanity's relation to its own ends or to itself as the "being of ends" (Kant). It is not the appellation of the self-management of rational humanity or of some definitive truth inscribed in the heaven of the Ideas. It is the appellation, the utterly inadequate appellation, of a humanity that finds itself exposed to the absence of any given end—a heaven, a future—but not less exposed to the infinite for that. Exposed, existing.

DEMOCRACIES AGAINST DEMOCRACY

AN INTERVIEW WITH ERIC HAZAN

JACQUES RANCIÈRE

You dissent from the view that today there isn't anyone who isn't an adherent, a firm supporter, of democracy. Perhaps it's because you conceive of democracy quite differently from the way most people do.

The answer is twofold. In the first place, it is indeed my position that democracy is irreducible to either a form of government or a mode of social life. Second, even granting the so-called ordinary sense of the word *democracy*, it is not in the least evident to me that democracy enjoys total unquestioning support. Things were different during the cold war, when it was democracy versus totalitarianism. But since the Berlin Wall fell, what we've witnessed in the countries we call "the democracies" has been a mistrustful and faintly or openly derisive attitude toward democracy. In *Hatred of Democracy* I tried to show that a large part of the dominant discourse is working in one way or another against democracy.[1] Take for example the debates in France surrounding the elections of 2002 or the referendum on the European constitution in 2005. We heard all this talk about the democratic catastrophe, about irresponsible individuals, about all these little consumers pondering great national choices as though they were shopping for perfume or something. What all this led to in the end was that the constitution was not resubmitted to the popular vote. Indeed we saw a huge display of distrust of the popular vote. Yet the popular vote is part of the official definition of democracy. We heard the same old line coming from people like Daniel Cohn-Bendit: that democracy brought Hitler to power and so on. Among those regarded as intellectuals the dominant view is that democracy is the rule of the preformatted individual consumer, it is mediocracy, the rule of the media. You find the same stance from the right to the far left, from Alain Finkielkraut to *Tikkun*.

Yet, for all that, everyone identifies as democratic . . .

Not at all! "The democracies" is just the conventional term for that bloc of states. Internally, the democrat is an enemy. The Trilateral Commission was pushing this line thirty years ago: democracy, by which they meant the uncontrolled activity of democrats, nobodies trying to get involved in public affairs, was a threat to the democracies, meaning the wealthy countries.

What we are seeing today takes us right back to the time when the word originated. Ever since, the one thing on which all have agreed is that *democracy* denotes different, opposing things. It starts with Plato, who says that democracy is not a form of government, just the whim of people who want to behave licentiously. It continues with Aristotle, who says that democracy is fine, as long as the democrats are kept from exercising it. And how many times in the modern era have we heard that old chestnut from Churchill about democracy being the worst regime, except for all the others? So I don't believe there is universal assent to democracy, only universal consensus that it means two different things.

Your position puts me in mind of a sort of triangle, with constitutional liberties in one corner, the parliamentary system in another, and in the third Rancièrean democ-

racy, the locus of the power of all those with no special entitlement to exercise it. Does a word that polysemic, covering things that different, deserve to be retained, or is it not worn out? Because words do get used up; republic is an example. In 1825 you could get your head chopped off for identifying as a "republican" in France, but today it is meaningless.

Being fought over is what makes a political notion properly political as I see it, not the fact that it has multiple meanings. The political struggle is also the struggle for the appropriation of words. There is an old philosophical dream, which analytic philosophy still keeps alive, of defining the meanings of words with such perfection as to make ambiguity and multiple meanings vanish . . . but I think the struggle over words is important, and that it is normal for "democracy" to refer to different things in context. For the average French intellectual, democracy is a shopper home from the supermarket, slumped in front of her TV. But I am just back from Korea, where there was dictatorship until twenty years ago and where the idea of a collective power separate from the machinery of the state is meaningful enough to make the people take to the street and occupy it in spectacular fashion. I quite accept that the word is somewhat the worse for wear in the West, where it was invented, but if you think about everything that is going on in Asia, the word still bears meaning. If there is a better word we can replace it with, fine. Egalitarianism isn't exactly the same thing. Democracy—that's the equality already there at the core of inequality. What word hasn't been torn and frayed by use? Then there's another serious problem: you have to know what you're doing before you decide to drop a word, what forces you might be activating or deactivating.

I wonder whether, for you, democracy, being neither a form of government nor a form of society, isn't an unattainable ideal. Or rather a critical tool, a polemical battering ram.

No, it's not an ideal, because I always follow the principle of Jacotot that equality is a presupposition, not a goal to be attained. What

I am trying to convey is that democracy, in the sense of the power of the people, the power of those who have no special entitlement to exercise power, is the very basis of what makes politics thinkable. If power is allotted to the wisest or the strongest or the richest, then it is no longer politics we are talking about. It's the argument of Rousseau: the power of the strongest need not present itself as a right—if the strongest is the strongest, he imposes his will, and that's all there is to it. No need for further legitimation. I think that democracy is an egalitarian presupposition from which even an oligarchic regime like the one we have has to seek some degree of legitimation. Yes, democracy does have a critical function: it is the wrench of equality jammed (objectively and subjectively) into the gears of domination, it's what keeps politics from simply turning into law enforcement.

On the last page of Hatred of Democracy, *you write "egalitarian society is no more than the ensemble of egalitarian relations spun into existence in the here and now through singular and precarious acts." That leads, in turn, democracy and politics being almost synonymous for you, to something you said in your* Theses on Politics: *"Politics comes about as an always provisional accident in the history of forms of domination." Or again, from the end of* Disagreement, *"Politics, in the fully specific sense, is rare. It is always local and provisional."² Precarious, provisional, and occasional—is that how you see politics and democracy? These sudden, brief upswellings leading nowhere . . . isn't that a bleak vision of movements of emancipation?*

I don't think I ever said anything about brief upsurges leading nowhere. I don't have a vision of history as punctuated equilibrium, where things erupt at intervals and then lapse back into platitude. In the text you cite, all I was trying to say was that equality exists as the ensemble of the practices that trace out its domain: there is no other reality of equality than the reality of equality. I didn't mean to suggest that equality exists only on the barricades, and that once the barricades come down it's over, and we go back to listlessness. I am not a thinker of the event, of the upsurge, but rather of emancipation as something with its own tradition, with a history that isn't just made up of great striking deeds, but also of the ongoing effort to create forms of the common different from the ones on offer from the state, the democratic consensus, and so on. Of course there are events that punctuate the flow, that open up temporalities. The three "July Days" of 1830, for example, opened up the historic terrain on which the workers' associations, the insurrections of 1848, and the Paris Commune later came to grief.

Equality exists through that, in actuality, and not as a goal we might reach if we had the right strategy or the right leadership or the right science. Frankly, I don't see why that stance is bleaker than any other. We all know what a proliferation there was of deep revolutionary thinkers in Italy, and the result? Berlusconi. One of these days we ought to call all these people who hold the key to the future, these political prognosticators, to account—make them account for what's going on right now. If they're the optimists and I'm the pessimist, if they're the realists and I'm the dreamer . . . *(laughs)*.

For someone like you who has worked a lot in the archives, I don't get the feeling that you are all that strongly oriented toward the past.

Yes. I believe there are traditions of emancipation. The one I try to work on, or work in, is different from the one that got confiscated by the strategic visionaries, Lenin and the like. I've always fought against the idea of historical necessity. As for working in the archives, from that I learned at any rate that history is made by people who have only one life. What I mean is, history isn't some entity that acts or speaks; what we call history is what is woven by people as they construct a situation in time out of their own lives and experiences. We retell the stories of collective subjects like the working class or the workers' movement, but everyone can see that the transmission gets interrupted from time to time; some threads of the past get ruptured, then heal and reform. Look at what happened subsequent to 1968. For years, stretching into decades, the 1960s were denigrated and even execrated. Then arrives a generation with a fresh interest in what was going on in the 1960s, who rediscover Maoism, and so on. Sooner or later a new generation arrives that tries to reinvest certain words with meaning, certain hopes linked to those words, but in different contexts and with differing, indeed aleatory, forms of transmission.

DEMOCRACY FOR SALE

KRISTIN ROSS

Cuchulain vs. Kouchner

Am I a democrat? "Democrat," at least for Auguste Blanqui writing in 1852, was a word, as he put it, "without definition": "What is a democrat, I ask you. This is a vague and banal word, without any precise meaning, a rubbery word."[1]

Is "democrat" an any less rubbery name to embrace in our own time?

In June 2008 Ireland, the only country to hold a popular referendum on the European constitution, voted to reject it. One of the principal authors of the treaty, Valéry Giscard d'Estaing, was the first to admit that the text of the treaty (which ran over 312 pages in the English language version) was little revised from the version the French and the Dutch had rejected three years earlier, when they too held a referendum by popular vote. "The tools were exactly the same.

They just had been rearranged in the tool box."[2] The same treaty, in other words, was being revoted, after having been rejected by the French and the Dutch. This time around it was a "quirk," as the mainstream media regularly called it, in the Irish constitution, which gave the Irish the right to approve or disapprove the treaty by popular vote when all the other countries, including now France and Holland, were to be represented by deputies. A mounting mood of suspicion toward the Irish vote was palpable in the European press, which viewed "the quirk" as a potential occasion for irrational and destructive behavior on the part of the public. The Irish, after all, like the third world, might lack the political sophistication to make the right choice; they might not be ready for democracy. The suspicion boiled over in the days immediately preceding the election when French foreign minister Bernard Kouchner took it upon himself to make clear to the Irish that they were, in effect, *obliged* to vote yes out of gratitude to a Europe that had dragged them out of the bogs. It would be, he stated, "very, very annoying for the right-thinking people ["la pensée honnête"] if we couldn't count on the Irish, who themselves have counted heavily on Europe's money."[3] The division he established between the Irish, cast now as brigands who had absconded with Brussels's cash, and *la pensée honnête,* presumably all other Europeans who have learned to regard politics as a giant intercountry game of treaties, summits, and committees, had been suggested a few days earlier by Daniel Cohn-Bendit: "The Irish have gotten everything from Europe, and they aren't conscious of it."[4]

The language of a "new" and technocratic Europe barely masked the repetition of colonialist tropes of older empires: the Irish figured as the latest rendition of the uneducated and unteachable people, whose appropriate response could only be gratitude to its leaders. But there was a new twist. Irish support for the constitution was viewed as an obligation of *repayment*; an investment, it seems, had been made, and the EU wanted a return on the investment. As President Sarkozy reportedly told his aides, "They [the Irish] are bloody fools. They have been stuffing their faces at European expense for years and now they dump us in the shit."[5]

The referendum was supposed to be nothing more than an exercise in rubber-stamping the experts' text. But the Irish decided to treat the vote as a real vote. In their decision to reject the treaty and their refusal to align themselves with the powerful nations, some heard an echo of Bandung: the Irish were constituting themselves not only as a minority, but as a different kind of minority: those whose recent history had been a colonial one. Others, after the election, expressed what they took to be a general explanation for the treaty's defeat: the reluctance of voters to approve something they had been told in advance they were incapable of understanding and should leave to their betters to administer. As one "No" voter put it, "the reason that the treaty went down to defeat is that we Irish voters found it to be an impenetrable read and an impossible thing to get our collective heads around. The Treaty was *purposefully drafted* to defy our understanding."[6] It was purposefully drafted, in other words, to communicate to voters through its very form that it was best to leave such complex matters of governance up to the experts, the technocracy.

EU officials were quick to blame "populism" for the defeat. The Irish, they insisted, must be made to *revote*, presumably until the correct result could be reached. Valéry Giscard d'Estaing and Nicolas Sarkozy immediately called for a new vote. Giscard went on the airways:

GISCARD: "The Irish must be allowed to express themselves again."

NICOLAS DEMORAND (the radio interviewer): "Don't you find it deeply shocking to make people who have already expressed themselves take the vote over?"

GISCARD: "We spend out time revoting. If we didn't, the president of the Republic would be elected for all eternity"[7]

Sometimes there is all the time in the world to vote again. After all, the Lisbon Treaty was itself a revote, after the French and Dutch had defeated it. Other times, as in the contested Bush/Gore U.S. election in 2000, there is no time to revote or even to recount existing votes. In the impoverished rural area in the Hudson Valley where I live, we indeed pass our time revoting. Our county ranks near the bottom—which is to say with counties in Mississippi and Alabama—in the mediocrity of its school system, a mediocrity measured in terms of the ratio of money spent per student and uniform test results. Our county spends the highest amount of money for the worst results. But on the rare occasions when voters manage to vote "No" on yet another inflated school budget proposal in an attempt to hold bureaucrats and administrators accountable, the same exact proposal, accompanied by a renewed chorus of warnings against "abandoning our kids," is put up for a vote month after month until it succeeds.

"Revoting," then, in today's actually existing representative democracies, is nothing unusual. "No," apparently, doesn't really mean no. What was striking about the aftermath of the Irish vote was not only that a treaty pronounced dead by popular vote was still very much alive, but that through exercising their democratic right to vote, by taking the election seriously, the Irish, in the view of the EU oligarchy, had struck a blow not against the powers of the Parliament, but *against democracy itself.* Here is Hans-Gert Pöttering, president of the European Parliament: "It is of course a great disappointment, for all those who wanted to achieve greater democracy, greater political effectiveness and greater clarity and transparency in decision-making in the EU, that the majority of the Irish could not be convinced of the need for these reforms of the EU."[8]

The proof, it seems, was in the numbers. 500 million Europeans had been taken hostage by 862,415 Irish—less than 0.2 percent of the European population. The leaders of the large nations, France and Germany, reacted:

AXEL SCHÄEFER (SPD leader in the German Bundestag): "We cannot allow the huge majority of Europe to be duped by a minority of a minority of a minority." [9]

WOLFGANG SCHAEUBLE (German interior minister): "A few million Irish cannot decide on behalf of 495 million Europeans." [10]

JEAN DANIEL: "A country of four or five million inhabitants can't hold countries made up of 490 million citizens hostage." [11]

Now, presumably among the 500 million Europeans held hostage by Irish banditry could be counted the French and Dutch who had themselves voted no on the constitution earlier. But we won't quibble over numbers. What is more interesting is to see the reappearance of a discursive figure, a familiar character, that made its debut during the most recent historic moment of high panic among the elites, the 1960s, and has been strategically conjured up at subsequent crisis moments: the "silent majority." When "the silent majority" appears, the world has been divided into two according to a quantitative logic whereby forces are presented in both numerical and moral terms: the "law" that a silent, reproachful, and now purportedly "oppressed" majority must defend against a stigmatized and vocal minority, a civic and majoritarian Europe hijacked by a subversive and destructive minority. The "silent majority" appears when the largest number is *spoken for* rather than speaks and when the voice of the minority is increasingly voided of authority and rendered illegitimate.[12]

Frédéric Bas has traced the invention of the term *the silent majority* back to the moment it originated in the mouths of Richard Nixon and Spiro Agnew as they attempted to counteract the noisy opposition to the Vietnam War out in the streets. In France the first use of the term, in the context of the passage of the *loi anticasseurs* in 1970, was, as Bas points out, inscribed in the framework of a general reflection on democracy: "In our democracy, it is the duty of each citizen to prevent minorities from imposing their law on the silent majority of the country. If that majority acts like sheep, it will awaken to the reign of the colonels or that of majority agitators who, without taking account of existing laws, will impose their own."

But it was none other than Valéry Giscard d'Estaing who Bas credits with introducing (in latent form) the figure in the midst of the May-June insurrections, on May 19, 1968, back when he was a deputy from Puy-de-Dome:

> In the grave national circumstances our country is undergoing, I want merely to express the point of view that I know to be that of the greatest number of students, workers, but also of French men and women everywhere. This majority wishes that order be restored and liberties be protected. . . . Up until now, the greatest number of French people, who love order, liberty, and progress, and who accept neither arbitrariness nor anarchy, have remained silent. If necessary, they must be ready to express themselves.

In the 1960s, the indeterminate silence of "the greatest number" could be confidently translated or ventriloquized by government officials as expressing a bastion of good sense against anarchy or arbitrariness. The minority had "seized speech" in the streets, but the *highly valorized* silence of the majority could function as a vast reserve army, a force held back until the moment when it would be called upon to express itself, in the legitimate way, that is: by voting. In 2008 the silent majority, the "greatest number" of Europeans, finds its silence just as confidently translated by the ruling elite, but its silence is now constrained to be eternal—democracy as voiceless assent. The situation is one in which those who are deprived of their political say function comfortably in the belief that "governability"— a concept massively promoted in the 1990s—benefits everyone, despite the fact that "governabilty" actually consists of the most unlimited wielding of power by the most powerful and wealthy classes. Indeed, another way of looking at the Irish referendum is that the Irish, invested with the specter of democracy as lawless or violent, were being asked to vote away their right, as well as everyone else's, to ever vote again, by helping force through a ruling bureaucracy insulated to a virtually impermeable degree against democratic accountability. The EU had made an investment in Ireland and the interest they required as a return on their investment was either the abrogation of the right to vote or what amounted to the same thing: the obligation to keep voting until the correct vote—assent—was obtained. Governability—the creation of faraway, supranational, European bureaucratic bodies against which no worker's organization can fight directly—is designed to prevent radical minorities in wealthy or overdeveloped societies from upsetting the system in any way.

In 1968, many of the minority engaged in direct democracy out on the streets viewed elections, the tired, ritualized exercise of representative democracy, as, in the famous words of Sartre, "a trap for fools." What the gap between our own time and the 1960s indicates is first of all a progressive dismantling of universal suffrage—the attempt to deprive even "representative" democracy of its validity in the effort to offset the unpleasant effects of universal suffrage and in favor of "rationalizing" people's will and the expression of that will. The term *consensus* is no longer adequate to describe what is in fact a kind of socializing of people into silence—silence as consent. But it also says something about the creative, bricolagelike capacity of the demos, when even a ballot box can become a weapon. It suggests that democracy can reassert itself via the most diverse of political forms. By taking an outmoded ritual seriously when, as Giscard's cynicism makes patently clear, no one else does, even voting, in this instance, can become an instantiation of "fugitive democracy": the political potentialities of ordinary citizens.[13] The vote could be treated as a weapon to be used in the antidemocratic assault on popular sovereignty by a "Europe" that presents itself as the reign of democracy on earth, a brand-name sold by evoking peace, justice, and above all, democracy.

Democracy for Sale

The modern, received understanding of democracy is rule by voting, the authority to decide matters by majority rule, the rule of "the greatest number." But another understanding of the term, familiar to readers of Jacques Rancière's *Le Maître ignorant,* conveys a sense of power that is neither quantitative nor concerned with control. It is rather one of potentiality or enablement: the capacity of ordinary people to discover modes of action for realizing common concerns. Rancière's encounter with Joseph Jacotot, and his continuing reworking of that encounter, have helped make available what was in fact the original, more expansive and suggestive, meaning of the word *democracy*: namely, the capacity to do things. Democracy is not a form of government. And it is not concerned with number—neither with a tyrannical majority nor a minority of agitators. In ancient Greece, as Josiah Ober points out, of the three major terms designating political power—*monarchia, oligarchia, and demokratia*—only *demokratia* is unconcerned with number. The *monos* of *monarchia* indicates solitary rule; the *hoi oligoi* of oligarchy indicates the power of a few. Only *demokratia* does not provide an answer to the question "how many?"[14] The power of the *demos* is neither the power of the population nor its majority but rather the power of anybody. Anybody is as entitled to govern as he or she is to be governed.

Yet if democracy as "the capacity to do things" is free from the law of number, it does presuppose an existing division of the world into two, a division between those who are defined as having the capacity to participate in collective decision making (the "best people") and those said to be without that capacity. Democracy *refuses* this division as the basis of organizing political life; it is a call for equality on the part of the people defined as not being among the best people. "The best" have been defined in different ways throughout history: as those who possess noble birth, the right race, those who exhibit military power, as the wealthy, or those who possess complex knowledge or managerial skills. And as Immanuel Wallerstein reminds us, the modes of defining who count among "the best" have always been accompanied by assumptions about the ethos or lifestyle of "the best people"—assumptions, for example, that a "civilized" nature is their particular endowment.[15]

When Blanqui in 1852 complained about the rubbery nature of the name *democrat,* he was already registering the profound modification the term was beginning to undergo—a modification that would last throughout the Second Empire and beyond. Up until then the word had largely retained its revolutionary 1789 heritage; *democrat* was the label, for example, of many far-left organizations in the 1830s and 1840s. But during the Second Empire the Imperial Regime had effectively appropriated the term for itself, for the most part successfully, by opposing what it called real "democracy" to the bourgeois "party of order."[16] The emperor, in other words, claimed to have given sovereignty back to the people by the "plebiscite" or the *appel au peuple.* Monarchists in the 1850s and 1860s embraced the word, equating it favorably with Empire; the minister of the interior, an impassioned Bonapartist, was able to call himself "the defender of democracy." By 1869, a partial enumeration of the kinds of "democrats" flourishing in French political life included *démocrates socialistes, démocrates révolutionnaires, démocrates bourgeois, démocrates impérialistes, démocrates progressistes,* and *démocrates autoritaires.* The list reflects both the point Blanqui was making—that the term was entirely up for grabs—as well as the effort made by some socialists to affirm the revolutionary heritage of the word by lending precision to their position with an appropriate qualifier. But the word on its own—then as today—

conveyed virtually no information. Blanqui was not the only Republican or socialist to hesitate to use a word his adversaries used to describe themselves. As he writes to Maillard:

> You say to me: "I am neither bourgeois, nor proletarian. I am a democrat. Beware of words without definition, they are the preferred instrument of schemers. . . . It is they who invented the beautiful aphorism: neither proletarian nor bourgeois, but democrat! . . . What opinion couldn't manage to find a home under that roof? Everyone claims to be a democrat, even aristocrats.

Democrat no longer named the division to be overcome between those judged capable of governing and those judged incapable: it was too rubbery, it did no labor, it created consensus rather than division. Even the Communards of 1871, engaged in their short-lived experiment in taking control of the administrative and institutional functions normally reserved for traditional elites, did not call themselves democrats. The declaration of the communal form of government in Paris in the wake of the French capitulation to the Prussians signified nothing if not the most renewed commitment to democratic politics in modern times. In their brief existence the Communards replaced long-entrenched hierarchic and bureaucratic structures with democratic forms and processes at every level. Yet these agents of democracy preferred other words—*républicains, peuple*—to describe themselves. But I think it is significant that they did not entirely abandon the word *démocratie*. Even though it had been derailed from its true meaning and had fallen into the hands of the enemy, it still retained the heritage of 1789.

When Arthur Rimbaud entitled one of his last prose poems "Démocratie," a poem written soon after the demise of the Commune, the title is nothing more than a banner under which a mobile and imperialistic bourgeois class expands out from the metropolis to the "languid, scented lands," feeding, as the poem says, "the most cynical whoring," "destroying all logical revolt."

Democracy

"Toward that intolerable country
The flag floats along
And the beating drums are stifled
By our rough backcountry shouting . . . "
"In the metropolis we will feed the most cynical whoring.
 We will destroy all logical revolt."
"On to the languid scented lands! In the service of the most
 monstrous industrial or military exploitations."
"Goodbye to all this, and never mind where."
Conscripts of good intention,
We will have savage philosophy;
Knowing nothing of science, depraved in our pleasures,
To hell with the world around us . . .
"This is the real advance! Forward. . March!"

What if it were Rimbaud, and not Baudelaire, whom we read as the poet that best compiled the central tropes and figures of the nineteenth century? With images courtesy of Edgar Allan Poe and Jules Verne, with prophecies drawn from political pamphlets, with figures taken from children's novels and popular science texts, Rimbaud assembles the emblems and possible futures of his moment. And the colonial soldier is very much one of those figures, producing as many, if not more, of the principal postures, orientations, stereotypes, and directions, as does the ragpicker or *flaneur* for the future of the twentieth and twenty-first centuries. "Démocratie" the poem, and the *Illuminations* taken as a group, stand on the brink, so to speak, of a mutating world system: their moment is the inauguration of a world drawn together by colonialism, the moment when a genuinely bourgeois regime begins to install itself definitively.[17] Just as significant, though, is what occurs immediately before the writing of these poems: the class massacre that occurred in the heart of "civilized Europe": the mass shootings of tens of thousands of Communards in May 1871. This attempt on the part of the bourgeois-republican government to physically exterminate one by one and *en bloc* its class enemy, to kill all those who had engaged in the brief attempt to change the political and social order, is quite extraordinary:

The executions were not just happening in the Luxembourg. They were shooting people down on the street corners, in the passageways between houses, against doors. Wherever they could find a wall to push victims up against.

The banks of the Seine were witness to ferocious massacres. Underneath the Pont Neuf they were executing people for eight days straight. In the afternoon, gentlemen and their ladies would come out to watch the prisoners being killed. Elegant couples attended the butchery as they would a play.

In a corner of the Left Bank that surrounds the neighborhood of the Pantheon, a half dozen courts-martial were functioning. The mass killings took place at the Luxembourg. But they were shooting people at the Monnaie, at l'Observatoire, at the law school, at the Ecole polytechnique, at the Pantheon. They were executing people at the Collège de France, based on condemnations pronounced by a provost seated in the room on the left of the main entrance. There were continuous executions in the Maubert market.

Six courts-martial for this one neighborhood. For each of them, more and more deaths. The Luxembourg alone counted more than a thousand. As they advanced, the Versaillais installed sinister military magistrates, one by one in each square, whose only task was to organize the killing. Judgment didn't matter.

Around the large slaughterhouses—the Luxembourg, the Ecole Militaire, the parc Monceau, La Roquette, the Père Lachaise, the Buttes Chaumont, and still others—countless massacres were conducted in a more muffled fashion, with less ostentatious display and less glory.[18]

I have quoted at length from this eyewitness account of the *semaine sanglante* because I think we should linger on the sheer magnitude of the hatred exhibited by the bourgeois-republican government, on what Luciano Canfora calls "the furious hostility of the *majority*."[19] For it was this class massacre, he reminds us, that was the defeat of democracy that gave birth to the Third Republic. In November of that year, Rimbaud and his friend Delahaye walked the streets of Paris, examining the traces of bullet holes left in the walls of houses and of the Pantheon; the months and, in fact, years after the massacre left a political atmosphere infused, as Rimbaud remarked to his friend, with "annihilation, chaos . . . all the possible and even probable *reactions*."[20] The *Illuminations* open onto the movement of late-nineteenth-century expansionism and the wholesale creation of a consciousness conducive to reproducing a colonialist expeditionary class this entailed. In certain of his more futuristic poems, Rimbaud foresees that movement culminating in a bland and homogeneous universe: "a little world, pale and flat" as he puts it in one poem, or in "the same bourgeois magic wherever your baggage sets you down." In others—I'm thinking here of "Métropolitain," "Barbare," and "Soir historique,"—he shows us some of the ways the bourgeois imagination intoxicates itself with apocalyptic images of its own death. In this second cluster of poems, Rimbaud presents the canceled future of a now vanished imperial destiny: a panoramic vision where crystalline and fantastic cityscapes rejoin ancient prefigurations of the end of the world in geological cataclysms of exploding ice and snow; intertwining bridges and highways lie flanked by barbarian tribes, a recurring planetary conflagration, at once polar and fiery, chaotic yet eerily still.

How can the future be imagined after the demise of the Commune? Having lived the eruption, evolution, and liquidation of that unusual experiment in democracy, faced now with the "swamp," as he called it, of the French middle classes consolidating the colonial impetus that would propel them through the next several decades, Rimbaud chooses to prefigure both the triumph and the death of that class in a series of futuristic and fantastic prose poems—the triumph of that class in a progressive homogenization of the planet, its death in an exploded earth.

Rimbaud's "Démocratie," then, marks the precise moment when the term *democracy* is no longer being used to express the demands of the *peuple* in a national class struggle, but is rather being used to *justify* the colonial policies of the "civilized lands" in a struggle on an international scale between the West and the rest, the civilized and the noncivilized. Rimbaud recounts that saga in the "Mauvais Sang" section of *Une Saison en enfer* and provides an additional class portrait of the civilizing missionaries in a poem called "Movement":

> These are the conquerors of the world,
> Seeking their personal chemical fortune:
> Sport and comfort accompany them;
> They bring education for races, for classes, for animals
> Within this vessel, rest and vertigo
> In diluvian light,
> In terrible evenings of study.

The resonance of democracy registered by Rimbaud was definitively changed, not merely diluted but filled with an alien content, as the very groups who feared it at the beginning of the century begin to embrace it at the century's end. As in Rimbaud's poem, democracy becomes a banner, a slogan, a proof of being civilized as well as the vital spiritual supplement, the ideal fig leaf, to the civilized and civilizing West. The State, in the name of representative democracy, inaugurates a history of class massacre, within Europe in the form of the Commune and beyond, in the colonial domains, a violence whose echoes can be heard in the language of threat and contempt directed at the Irish at the time of the 2008 vote. The West, as democratic, can become the world's moral leader, since its hegemony is the basis of progress throughout the world. From these "conquerors of the world" to Woodrow Wilson's "making the world safe for democracy" and onto Harry Truman's recoding of *democracy* into the language and project of development economics requires no leap at all.[21]

But before we leave Rimbaud's prefiguration of world history, we must consider, in the context of "Democracy," and "Movement," a poem that may have much to say to our own historical moment, the poem structured as one long advertising spiel entitled "Sale." In an atmosphere made up of equally modern and magical installations, the poem presents the revolutionary cry and the advertising slogan as indistinguishable from each other in a generalized onslaught of consumer goods and services: "For sale—Priceless bodies, beyond race or world or sex or lineage!" Both "Sale" and "Democracy" relate changes in consciousness to the relative penetration of market relationships into everyday life—whether these be in the *outremer* colonies or in the heart of the European metropolis. (A sonnet written around this time, entitled "Paris," consists entirely of advertising pitches lifted off of Parisian storefronts.) What might be called the prophetic or extraordinarily contemporary feel of these poems—read together, they amount to the title of this chapter, "Democracy for Sale"—has something to do with the way the twentieth century solidified the equation between democracy (in its inverted form) and consumption begun in Rimbaud's time: democracy as the right to buy. Today's Western liberal democracies are all the more assured in their well-being in that they are more perfectly depoliticized, lived as a kind of falsely timeless ambience, a milieu or style of existence. And this is the atmosphere envisioned by Rimbaud in "Sale": the free exchange of merchandise, bodies, candidates, lifestyles, and possible futures. "For sale—Homesteads and migrations, sports, enchantments and perfect comfort, and the noise, the movement and the future they entail!"

Today, democracy is the slogan of almost all of the leaders on the planet (and the rest, sooner or later, will be brought forcibly into the fold). What separates our own time from the extraordinary moment of Rimbaud is something called the cold war and its ending. In terms of the development of "democracy," it is difficult to overestimate the enormous gain Western governments managed to consolidate when they successfully advanced *democracy* as the opposing counterweight to *communism*. They had actually gained control of the entire word for themselves, leaving nary a trace of its former emancipatory resonance. Indeed, democracy had become a class ideology justifying systems that allowed a very small number of people to govern—and to govern without the people, so to speak; systems that seem to exclude any other possibility than the infinite reproduction of their own functioning. To be able to call an unchecked and deregulated free market economy, a ruthless, no-holds-barred opposition to communism, a right to intervene, militarily and otherwise, in countless sovereign nations and their internal affairs—to succeed in calling all this democracy was an incredible feat. To manage to make the market be considered as an evident condition of democracy and to have democracy viewed as inexorably calling forth the market, is an astounding accomplishment. It was considerably helped along, in France, at least, in the reaction against the '68 years, as the French Revolution, under the profoundly antidemocratic tutelage of François Furet, was submitted to a patient labor of inconsideration, denigrated in comparison to the acceptable revolution of 1776 and ultimately affiliated to Stalinism and the crimes of Pol Pot. And, with the end of "actually existing socialism," we at last, it seemed, finished definitively with moments of rupture or conflict, and society could be from now on the place for uninterrupted "democratic" deliberation, dialogue, debate, and a perpetual regulation of social relations. Rimbaud's moment, as we have seen in "Democracy," initiated the age of "democratic empire": a natural, inevitable project designed to bring about a predestined future of the peoples or entities being developed. But "democracy" is just as much at work, as we saw in "Sale," on the homefront: where the main system of rule in a society is the economy, a vast historic force beyond human power, and where a silent consensus informs us that the equilibrium produced by the economy defines the best of all possible worlds.

Is this a permanent contamination of the language of politics? Can I call myself a democrat?

It's certainly not enough to criticize, in an incrementalist way, the "failed" or "insufficient" democracy of this or that law, party, or state. To do so is to remain enclosed in a system that is perfectly happy to critique, say, the blatant seizure of electoral procedures by a Robert Mugabe in Zimbabwe, but remains powerless before the same process when it is accomplished by economic phenomena that respect democratic rituals—like the exactions of the IMF, for example. In fact, the understanding of democracy as having to do with elections or with the will of the majority is a very recent historical understanding. What is called representational democracy—in our own time said to consist of free elections, free political parties, a free press, and, of course, the free market—is in fact an oligarchic form: representation by a minority granted the title of stewards or trustees of common affairs. All today's "advanced industrial democracies" are in fact oligarchic democracies: they represent the victory of a dynamic oligarchy, a world government centered on great wealth and the worship of wealth, but capable of building consensus and legitimacy through elections that, by limiting the range of options, effectively protect the ascendancy of the middle and upper classes.[22]

I think we must both recognize this to be the case, that is, recognize the nonexistence of democracy or its inversion in reality, at the same time that we acknowledge how vitally necessary it is to retain the original, expansive sense of the term. If we remain enclosed in an understanding of democracy as a form of government, then we have no choice but to abandon the word to the enemy who has appropriated it. But precisely because it is not a form of government, because it is not a type of constitution or institution, democracy, as the power of anybody to concern himself or herself with common affairs, becomes another name for the specificity of politics itself. It may exist or not exist at all, and it may reassert itself in the most varied of manifestations. It is a moment, at best a project rather than a form. As the name of the struggle against the perpetual privatization of public life, democracy, like love in one of Rimbaud's many slogans, must be reinvented.

FROM DEMOCRACY TO DIVINE VIOLENCE

SLAVOJ ŽIŽEK

I

In today's era, which proclaims itself postideological, ideology is thus more than ever a field of struggle—among other things, the struggle for appropriating past traditions. One of the clearest indications of our predicament is the liberal appropriation of Martin Luther King, in itself an exemplary ideological operation. Henry Louis Taylor recently remarked: "Everyone knows—even the smallest kid knows about Martin Luther King—can say his most famous moment was that 'I have a dream' speech. No one can go further than one sentence. All we know is that this guy had a dream. We don't know what that dream was." King had come a long way from the crowds who cheered him at the 1963 March on Washington, when he was introduced as "the moral leader of our nation": by taking on issues outside segregation, he had lost much of the public support and was more and more considered to be a pariah. He took on issues of poverty and militarism because he considered them vital to make equality something real and not just racial brotherhood but equality in fact. To put it in Badiou's terms, King followed the "axiom of equality" well beyond the topic of racial segregation: he was working on antipoverty and antiwar issues at the time of his death. He had spoken out against the Vietnam War and was in Memphis when he was killed in April 1968 in support of striking sanitation workers. Following King meant following the unpopular road, not the popular one. Today the equality between whites and blacks is celebrated as part of the American Dream, perceived as a self-evident politico-ethical axiom—however, in the 1920s and 1930s the Communists were the ONLY political force that argued for complete equality between the races.

So let me dive into the deep water of ideology and directly address the problem of democracy. When one is accused of undermining democracy, one's answer should thus be a paraphrase of the reply to the similar reproach (that communists are undermining family, property, freedom, etc.) in *The Communist Manifesto*: the ruling order itself is already undermining them. In the same way that (market) freedom is unfreedom for those selling their working force, in the same way family is undermined by the bourgeois family as legalized prostitution, democracy is undermined by its parliamentary form, with its concomitant passivization of the large majority as well as the growing executive privileges implied by the spreading logic of emergency state.

In the fall of 2007 a public debate was raging in the Czech Republic: although a large majority of people (around 70 percent) were opposed to the installation of U.S. Army radars on their territory, the government went on with the project. Government representatives rejected calls for a referendum, claiming that one does not decide with voting about such a sensitive national security matter—it should be left to military experts. (Interestingly, the same representatives evoked a purely political reason for the decision: the U.S. helped the

Czechs three times in their history to achieve freedom (1918, 1945, 1989), so now Czechs should return the favor . . .) If one follows this logic to the end, one arrives at a strange result: what then IS there to vote about? Should economic decisions not also be left to economic experts, etc.?

This brings us to the important topic of the blurred relationship between power and knowledge in modern societies. Jacques Lacan's originality in dealing with the couple knowledge/power was little noticed: in contrast to Foucault, who endlessly varied the motif of their conjunction (knowledge is not neutral, it is in itself an apparatus of power and control), Lacan insists on the disjunction between knowledge and power—in our era, knowledge has assumed a disproportionate growth in relationship to the effects of power. There are many ways to read this thesis. First, one can read it as stating an obvious, although often ignored, fact: we get to know more things much faster, and we do not know what to do about them. The prospect of ecological crisis is paradigmatic here: what if what makes us unable to act is not the fact that we "do not yet know enough" (is human industry really responsible for global warming, etc.), but, on the contrary, the fact that we know too much and do not know what to do with this mass of inconsistent knowledge, how to subordinate it to a Master-Signifier? This brings us to a more pertinent level, that of the tension between S1 and S2: the chain of knowledge is no longer totalized/quilted by Master-Signifiers. The exponential uncontrollable growth of scientific knowledge concerns drive as acephalous. Thus push-to-knowledge unleashes a "power that is not that of mastery": a power proper to the exercise of knowledge as such. The Church sensed this lack, quickly offering itself as the Master that will guarantee the explosion of scientific knowledge will remain within "human limits" and not overwhelm us—a vain hope, of course.

How right Lacan is when he sees modernity as the rise of the "university discourse" becomes clear when we focus on the phrase "to serve the people": not only is the leader legitimized by serving the people, the king himself has to reinvent his function as the "highest servant of the people" (as Frederick the Great put it). What is crucial is that there is no one who does not serve, but is simply being served: ordinary people serve the state or the People, the state itself serves the people. This logic reaches its climax in Stalinism where the entire population serves: ordinary workers are supposed to sacrifice their well-being for their community, the leaders work night and day, serving the people (although their "truth" is S1, the Master-Signifier) . . . The agency being served, People, has no substantial positive existence: it is the name for the abyssal Moloch every existing individual serves. The price of this paradox is, of course, a set of self-referential paradoxes: the people as individuals serve themselves as People, and their Leaders directly embody their universal interest as People, etc. The refreshing thing would have been to find individuals ready to naively adopt the position of the Master, simply claiming "I AM the one you are serving!" without this position of a Master being alienated in the knowledge of their Servants-Leaders.

2

The case of China is exemplary of this deadlock of democracy. Faced with today's explosion of capitalism in China, analysts often ask when political democracy as the "natural" political accompaniment of capitalism will enforce itself. However, a closer analysis quickly dispells this hope.

Instead of perceiving what goes on in today's China as an oriental-despotic distortion of capitalism, one should see in it the repetition of the development of capitalism in Europe itself. In early modernity most European states were far from democratic—if they were democratic (as was the case of the Netherlands), it was only for the liberal elite, not for the workers. Conditions for capitalism were created and sustained by a brutal state dictatorship, very much like today's China: the state legalizing violent expropriations of common people, which made them proletarians, and disciplining them in their new role. All the features we identify today with liberal democracy and freedom (trade unions, universal vote, free universal education, freedom of the press, etc.) were won in a long, difficult struggle of the lower classes throughout the nineteenth century, they were far from a natural consequence of capitalist relations. Recall the list of demands with which *The Communist Manifesto* concludes: most of them, but for the abolition of private property with the means of production, are today widely accepted in "bourgeois" democracies—the result of popular struggles.

Recall another ignored fact: today, the equality between whites and blacks is celebrated as part of the American Dream, perceived as a self-evident politico-ethical axiom—however, in the 1920s and 1930s the Communists were the ONLY political force that argued for complete equality between the races. Those who advocate the natural link between capitalism and democracy cheat in the same way the Catholic Church is cheating when it presents itself as the natural advocate of democracy and human rights against the threat of totalitarianism—as if the Church had not accepted democracy only at the end of the nineteenth century, and even this with teeth clenched, as a desperate compromise, making it clear that it preferred monarchy and that this was a concession to new times. The Catholic Church as a beacon of the respect for freedom and human dignity? Let us make a simple mental experiment. Until the early 1960s the Church maintained the (in)famous index of works whose reading was prohibited to (ordinary) Catholics; one could only imagine how the artistic and intellectual history of modern Europe might look if we erased from it all works that, at one time or another, found themselves on this index—a modern Europe without Descartes, Spinoza, Leibniz, Hume, Kant, Hegel, Marx, Nietzsche, Kafka, Sartre, not to mention the large majority of modern literary classics.

There is thus nothing exotic in today's China: what happens there merely repeats our own forgotten past. So what about the afterthought of some Western liberal critics: how much faster would China's development have been had it been combined with political democracy? In a TV interview a couple of years ago, Ralf Dahrendorf linked the growing distrust in democracy to the fact that, after every revolutionary change, the road to new prosperity leads through a "valley of tears": after the breakdown of socialism, one cannot directly pass to the abundance of a successful market economy—the limited, but real, socialist welfare and security had to be dismantled, and these first steps are necessarily painful; and the same goes for Western Europe, where the passage from the Welfare State to new global economy involves painful renunciations, less security, less guaranteed social care. For Dahrendorf, the problem is best encapsulated by the simple fact that this painful passage through the "valley of tears" lasts longer than the average period between (democratic) elections, so that the temptation is great to postpone the difficult changes for short-term electoral gains. Paradigmatic here is the disappointment of the large strata of postcommunist nations with the economic results of the new democratic order: in the glorious days of 1989 they equated democracy with the abundance of Western consumerist societies and now, ten years later, when the abundance is still missing, they blame democracy itself . . . Unfortunately, he focuses much less on the opposite temptation: if the majority resists the necessary structural changes in economy, would (one of) the logical conclusion(s) not be that, for a decade or so, an enlightened elite should take power, even by nondemocratic means, to enforce the necessary measures and thus lay the foundations for a truly stable democracy? Along these lines, Fareed Zakaria points out how democracy can only "catch on" in economically developed countries: if the developing countries are "prematurely democratized," the result is a populism that ends in economic catastrophe and political despotism—no wonder today's most economically successful Third World countries (Taiwan, South Korea, Chile) embraced full democracy only after a period of authoritarian rule.

Is this line of reasoning not the best argument for the Chinese way to capitalism as opposed to the Russian way? After the collapse of communism, Russia adopted a "shock therapy" and threw itself directly into democracy and the fast track to capitalism—with economic bankruptcy the result. (There are good reasons to be modestly paranoiac here: were the Western economic advisers to Yeltsin who proposed this way really as innocent as they appeared, or were they serving U.S. interests by weakening Russia economically?) The Chinese, on the contrary, followed the path of Chile and South Korea, using unencumbered authoritarian state power to control the social costs of the passage to capitalism, thus avoiding the chaos. In short, the weird combination of capitalism and communist rule, far from a ridiculous anomaly, proved a blessing (not even) in disguise; China developed so fast not in spite of authoritarian communist rule but because of it. So, to conclude with a Stalinist-sounding suspicion: what if those who worry about the lack of democracy in China really worry about the fast development of China that makes it the next global superpower, threatening Western primacy?

Even a further paradox is at work here: beyond all the cheap jibes and superficial analogies exists a profound structural homology between the Maoist permanent self-revolutionizing, the permanent struggle against the ossification of State structures, and the inherent dynamics of capitalism. Here one is tempted to paraphrase Bertolt Brecht's pun "What is the robbing of a bank compared to the founding of a new bank?": what are the violent and destructive outbursts of a Red Guardist caught in the Cultural Revolution compared to the true Cultural Revolution, the permanent dissolution of all life-forms necessitated by capitalist reproduction? Today the tragedy of the Great Leap Forward repeats itself as the comedy of the rapid capitalist Great Leap Forward into modernization, with the old slogan "iron foundry into every village" reemerging as "a skyscraper into every street."

So what about a quasi-Leninist defense of the Chinese capitalist explosion as a big prolonged case of NEP (the New Economic Politics, adopted by the Soviet Union, destroyed at the end of the civil war in 1921, which allowed private property and market exchange and lasted roughly till 1928), with the Communist Party firmly exerting political control, able at any moment to step in and undo its concessions to the class enemy? All one can do is bring this logic to its extreme: insofar as there is a tension in capitalist democracies between the democratic-egalitarian sovereignty of the people and the class divisions of the economic sphere, and insofar as the state can in principle enforce expropriations, etc., is not capitalism as such in a way one big NEP detour on a road that should pass directly from feudal or slave relations of domination to communist egalitarian justice?

And what if the promised democratic second stage that follows the authoritarian valley of tears never arrives? This, perhaps, is what is so unsettling about today's China: the suspicion that its authoritarian capitalism is not merely a reminder of our past, the repetition of the process of capitalist accumulation that, in Europe, went on from the sixteenth to eighteenth centuries, but a sign of the future? What if "the vicious combination of the Asian knout and the European stock market" proves itself to be economically more efficient than our liberal capitalism? What if it signals that democracy, as we understand it, is no longer a condition and driver of economic development, but its obstacle?

3

So where does this limitation of democracy become directly palpable? One cannot miss the irony of the fact that the name of the emancipatory political movement that suffered this international pressure is *Lavalas*—"flood" in Creole: it is the flood of the expropriated overflowing the gated communities. This is why the title of Peter Hallward's book on the overthrow of Aristide—*Damming the Flood*—is quite appropriate, inscribing the Haitian events into the global tendency of new dams and walls popping out everywhere after 9/11, confronting us with the truth of "globalization," the inner lines of division that sustain it.

Haiti was an exception from the very beginning, from its very revolutionary fight against slavery that ended in independence in January 1804: "Only in Haiti was the declaration of human freedom universally consistent. Only in Haiti was this declaration sustained at all costs, in direct opposition to the social order and economic logic of the day." For that reason, "there is no single event in the whole of modern history whose implications were more threatening to the dominant global order of things." The Haitian Revolution truly deserves the title of the *repetition* of the French Revolution: led by Toussaint l'Ouverture, it was clearly "ahead of its time," "premature," and doomed to fail, yet, precisely as such, it was perhaps even more of an Event than the French Revolution itself. It was the first time that the colonized rebelled not on behalf of returning to their precolonial "roots" but on behalf of the very modern principles of freedom and equality. And the sign of the Jacobins' authenticity is that they immediately recognized the slaves' uprising—the black delegation from Haiti was enthusiastically received in the National Assembly. (As expected, things changed after the Thermidor: Napoleon quickly sent the army to reoccupy Haiti.)

For this reason, the threat resided in the "mere existence of an independent Haiti," pronounced already by Talleyrand "a horrible spectacle for all white nations." Haiti HAD thus to be made an exemplary case of economic failure, to dissuade other countries from taking the same path. The price—LITERAL price—of the "premature" independence was horrible: after two decades of embargo,

France, the previous colonial master, established trade and diplomatic relations only in 1825, and for this Haiti had to agree to pay the sum of 150 million francs as a "compensation" for the loss of its slaves. This sum, roughly equal to the French annual budget at the time, was later cut to 90 million, but it continued to be a heavy burden that prevented any economic growth: at the end of the nineteenth century Haiti's payments to France consumed around 80 percent of the national budget, and the last installment was paid in 1947. When, in 2004, celebrating the bicentennial of the independence, the Lavalas president Jean-Baptiste Aristide demanded that France return this extorted sum, his claim was flatly rejected by a French commission (whose member was also Regis Debray)—so while U.S. liberals ponder the possibility of reimbursing U.S. blacks for slavery, Haiti's demand to be reimbursed for the tremendous amount the ex-slaves had to pay to have their freedom recognized was ignored by liberal opinion, even if the extortion here was double: the slaves were first exploited, then had to pay for the recognition of their hard-won freedom.

The story goes on today: what is for most of us a fond childhood memory—making mud cakes—is as desperate reality in Haiti slums like Cité Soleil. According to a recent AP report, a rise in food prices gave a new boost to a traditional Haitian remedy for hunger pangs: cookies made of dried yellow dirt. The mud, which has long been prized by pregnant women and children as an antacid and source of calcium, is considerably cheaper than real food: dirt to make one hundred cookies now costs five dollars. Merchants truck it from the country's central plateau to the market, where women buy it, process it into mud cookies, and leave them to dry under the scorching sun; the finished cookies are carried in buckets to markets or sold on the streets.

It is interesting to note that U.S.-French cooperation in overthrowing Aristide took place soon after the public discord about the attack on Iraq and was quite appropriately celebrated as the reaffirmation of the basic alliance that underlies their occasional conflicts; even Brazil's Lula, Toni Negri's hero, condoned the 2004 overthrow of Aristide. An unholy alliance was thus put together to discredit the Lavalas government as mob rule violating human rights, and President Aristide as a power-mad fundamentalist dictator—from illegal mercenary death squads and U.S.-sponsored "democratic fronts" to humanitarian NGOs and even some "radical left" organizations, financed by the U.S., that denounced Aristide's "capitulation" to IMF . . . Aristide himself provided a perspicuous characterization of this overlapping between radical left and liberal right: "somewhere, somehow, there's a little secret satisfaction, perhaps an unconscious satisfaction, in saying things that powerful white people want you to say." In short, the ruling ideology often remains the left's Ego-Ideal.

4

The case of Haiti also enables us to throw new light on the big (defining) problem of Western Marxism, that of the missing revolutionary subject: how is it that the working class does not complete the passage from in-itself to for-itself and constitute itself as a revolutionary agent? This problem provided the main raison d'être of its reference to psychoanalysis, which was evoked precisely to explain the unconscious libidinal mechanisms that prevent the rise of class consciousness inscribed into the very being (social situation) of the working class. In this way the truth of the Marxist socioeconomic analysis was saved, there was no reason to give ground to the "revisionist" theories about the rise of the middle classes, etc. For this same reason, Western Marxism was also in a constant search for other social agents who could play the role of revolutionary agent, as the understudy replacing the indisposed working class: third world peasants, students, and intellectuals, the excluded . . .

Therein resides the core of truth of Peter Sloterdijk's thesis, according to which the idea of Judgment Day, when all accumulated debts will be fully paid and an out-of-joint world will finally be set straight, is taken over in secularized form by the modern leftist project, where the agent of judgment is no longer God, but the people. Leftist political movements are like "banks of rage": they collect rage investments from people and promise them large-scale revenge, the reestablishment of global justice. Since, after the revolutionary explosion of rage, full satisfaction never takes place and an inequality and hierarchy reemerge, a push always arises for the *second*—true, integral—revolution that will satisfy the disappointed and truly finish the emancipatory work: 1792 after 1789, October after February . . . The problem is simply that there is never enough rage capital. That is why it is necessary to borrow from or combine with other rages: national or cultural. In fascism the national rage predominates; Mao's communism mobilizes the rage of exploited poor farmers, not proletarians. In our own time, when this global rage has exhausted its potential, two main forms of rage remain: Islam (the rage of the victims of capitalist globalization) plus "irrational" youth outbursts, to which one should add Latino American populism, ecologists, anticonsumerists, and other forms of antiglobalist resentment: the Porto Allegre movement failed to establish itself as a global bank for this rage, since it lacked a positive alternate vision.

The failure of the working class as revolutionary subject already lies in the very core of the Bolshevik revolution: Lenin's art was to detect the "rage potential" of disappointed peasants. The October Revolution was victorious because of the slogan "land and peace," addressed to the vast peasant majority, seizing the short moment of their radical dissatisfaction. Lenin was already thinking along these lines a decade earlier, which is why he was horrified at the prospect of the success of the Stolypin land reforms aimed at creating a new strong class of independent farmers—he wrote that if Stolypin succeeded, the chance for a revolution would be lost for decades.

All successful socialist revolutions, from Cuba to Yugoslavia, followed this model, seizing the opportunity in an extreme critical situation, co-opting the national-liberation or other "rage capitals." Of course, a partisan of the logic of hegemony would here point out that this is the very "normal" logic of revolution, that the "critical mass" is reached precisely and only through a series of equivalences among multiple demands that is always radically contingent and dependent on a specific—unique even—set of circumstances. A revolution never occurs when all antagonisms collapse into the big One, but when they synergetically combine their power . . . But the problem is here more complex: the point is not just that revolution no longer rides the train of History, following its Laws, since there is no History, since history is a contingent open process; the problem is a different one: it is as if there IS a Law of History, a more or less clear predominant main line of historical development, and that revolution can only occur in its interstices, "against the current." Revolutionaries have to wait patiently for the (usually very brief) period of time when the system openly malfunctions or collapses, seize the window of opportunity, grab the power, which at that moment, as it were, lies on the street, IS for grabs, and then fortify their hold on power, building repressive apparatuses, etc., so that, once the moment of confusion is over, the majority gets sober and is disappointed by the new regime, it is too late to get rid of it; they are firmly entrenched. The case of the communist ex-Yugoslavia is typical here: throughout World War II the communists ruthlessly hegemonized the resistance against the German occupying forces, monopolizing their role of antifascist struggle by way of actively trying to destroy all alternate ("bourgeois") resisting forces, while, simultaneously, strictly denying the communist nature of their struggle (if someone formulated the suspicion that they had plans to grab power and enact a communist revolution at war's end, he was swiftly denounced as spreading enemy propaganda). After the war, once they grabbed complete power, things swiftly changed and the regime openly displayed its communist nature. The communists, although genuinely popular till around 1946, nonetheless almost openly cheated in the 1946 general elections; when they were asked why they were doing it, since they could also have easily won free elections, their answer (in private, of course) was that this was true, but they would have lost the NEXT elections four years later, so it was better to make certain from the start what kind of elections they were ready to tolerate—in short, they were fully aware of the unique opportunity that brought them to power. The awareness of their failure to build and sustain a genuine long-term hegemony of popular support was thus from the very beginning taken into account.

Today one should shift this perspective totally and break the circle of such patient waiting for the unpredictable opportunity of social disintegration opening up the brief chance of grabbing power. Maybe—just maybe—this desperate waiting and *search* for the revolutionary agent is the form of appearance of its very opposite, the fear of *finding* it, of seeing it where it already bulges. For example, what about the fact that, today, the members-only phenomenon is exploding into a whole way of life, encompassing everything from private banking conditions to invitation-only health clinics: those with money are increasingly locking their entire lives behind closed doors. Rather than attend media-heavy events, they arrange private concerts, fashion shows, and art exhibitions in their own homes. They shop after-hours, and have their neighbors (and potential friends) vetted for class and cash. A new global class is thus emerging with, say, an Indian passport, a castle in Scotland, a pied-à-terre in New York, and a private Caribbean island—the paradox is that the members of this global class dine privately, shop privately, view art privately—everything is private. They are thus creating a lifeworld of their own to solve their hermeneutic problem—as Todd Millay says, "wealthy families can't just invite people over and expect them to understand what it's like to have $300 million." So what ARE their contacts with the world at large? Double, as expected: business plus humanitarianism (environment, fighting diseases, supporting arts . . .). The global citizens live their lives mostly in pristine nature—trekking in Patagonia, swimming on private islands. One cannot but note that the basic life-attitude of these gated superrich is *fear*: fear of external social life itself. The highest priorities of the "ultrahigh-networth individuals" are thus how to keep security risks—diseases, exposure to violent crime threats—at a minimum.

So aren't these "global citizens" living in secluded areas the true counterpole to those living in slums and other "white spots" of the public space? They are the two faces of the same coin, the two extremes of the new class division. The city that comes closest to this division is São Paolo in Lula's Brazil: a city with 250 heliports in its central downtown area. In order to insulate themselves from the dangers of mingling with ordinary people, the rich prefer to use helicopters, so that, when one looks around in São Paolo, one effectively feels like being in a futuristic city out of films like *Blade Runner* and *The Fifth Element*: ordinary people swarming the dangerous streets down on earth, the rich moving around on a higher level, in the air.

5

So, back to Haiti, the Lavalas struggle is exemplary of a principled heroism and the limitations of what can be done today: it didn't withdraw into the interstices of state power and "resist" from there, it heroically assumed state power, well aware that they are taking power in the most unfavorable circumstances, when all the trends of capitalist "modernization" and "structural readjustments," but also of the postmodern left, were against them—where was Negri's voice, otherwise celebrating Lula's rule in Brazil? Constrained by the measures imposed by the U.S. and IMF that were destined to enact "necessary structural readjustments," Aristide combined a politics of small and precise pragmatic measures (building schools and hospitals, creating infrastructure, raising minimal wages) with occasional acts of popular violence, reacting to military gangs—the single most controversial thing about Aristide, which earned him comparisons with Sendero Luminoso or Pol Pot, is his occasional condoning of *Pere Lebrun* (a form of popular self-defense: "necklacing," killing a police assassin or an informer with a burning tire; the name ironically refers to a local tire dealer; later the term stood for all forms of popular violence). In a speech on August 4, 1991, he advised an enthusiastic crowd to remember "when to use it and where to use it." Liberals immediately draw the parallel between *chimeres*, the Lavalas popular self-defense units, and *tonton macoutes*, the notorious murderous gangs of the Duvalier dictatorship—their preferred strategy is always the one of equating leftist and rightist "fundamentalists" so that, as with Simon Critchley, al Qaeda becomes a new reincarnation of the Leninist party, etc. Asked about *chimeres*, Aristide said: "the very word says it all. *Chimeres* are people who are impoverished, who live in a state of profound insecurity and chronic unemployment. They are the victims of structural injustice, of systematic social violence. . . . It's not surprising that they should confront those who have always benefited from this same social violence."

These desperate acts of violent popular self-defense were examples of what Benjamin called "divine violence": they are to be located "beyond good and evil" in a kind of politico-religious suspension of the ethical. Although we are dealing with what, to an ordinary moral consciousness, cannot but appear as "immoral" acts of killing, *one has no right to condemn them*, since they replied to years—centuries even—of systematic state and economic violence and exploitation. Jean Améry made this very point, referring to Frantz Fanon:

"I was my body and nothing else: in hunger, in the blow that I suffered, in the blow that I dealt. My body, debilitated and crusted with filth, was my calamity. My body when it tensed to strike, was my physical and metaphysical dignity. In situations like mine, physical violence is the sole means for restoring a disjointed personality. In the punch I was myself—for myself and for my opponent. What I later read in Frantz Fanon's *Les damnés de la terre,* in a theoretical analysis of the behaviour of colonised peoples, I anticipated back then when I gave concrete form to my dignity by punching a human face."

And the same point was made by none other than Hegel. When Hegel emphasizes how society—the existing social order—is the ultimate space in which the subject finds his substantial content and recognition, i.e., how subjective freedom can actualize itself only in the rationality of the universal ethical order, the implied (although not explicitly stated) obverse is that those who do NOT find this recognition have also the right to rebel: if a class of people is systematically deprived of their rights, of their very dignity as persons, they are *eo ipso* also released from their duties toward the social order, because this order is no longer their ethical substance—or, to quote Robin Wood: "When a social order fails to actualize its own ethical principles, that amounts to the self-destruction of those principles." Wood is fully justified in pointing out how the dismissive tone of Hegel's statements about the "rabble" should not blind us to the basic fact that he considered their rebellion rationally fully justified: the "rabble" is a class of people to whom systematically, not just in a contingent way, recognition by the ethical substance is denied, so they also do not owe anything to society, are dispensed of any duties toward it. As is well known, this is the starting point of the Marxian analysis: the "proletariat" designates such an "irrational" element of the "rational" social totality, its unaccountable "part of no part," the element systematically generated by it and, simultaneously, denied the basic rights that define this totality.

So what is divine violence? Its place can be defined in a very precise formal way. Badiou already elaborated the constitutive excess of representation over the represented: at the level of the Law, the state Power only represents the interests, etc. of its subjects; it is serving them, responsible to them, and itself subjected to their control; however, at the level of the superego underside, the public message of responsibility, etc., is supplemented by the obscene message of un-conditional exercise of Power: laws do not really bind me, I can do to you WHATEVER I WANT, I can treat you as guilty if I decide to do so, I can destroy you if I say so . . . This obscene excess is a *necessary* constituent of the notion of sovereignty—the asymmetry is here structural, i.e., the law can only sustain its authority if subjects hear in it an echo of the obscene unconditional self-assertion. And the people's "divine violence" is correlative to this excess of power: it is its counterpart—it targets this excess and undermines it.

6

The alternative "either struggle for state power (which makes us the same as the enemy we are fighting) or withdrawal to a resistance from a distance towards the state" is a false one—both its terms share the same premise: that a state-form, the way we know it, is here to stay, so that all we can do is take over the state or maintain a distance toward it. Here one should shamelessly repeat the lesson of Lenin's *State and Revolution*: the goal of revolutionary violence is not to take over the state power but to transform it, radically changing its func-tioning, its relation to its base, etc. Therein resides the key compo-nent of the "dictatorship of the proletariat"—Bulent Somay (per-sonal communication) was right to point out that what qualifies the proletariat for this position is ultimately a *negative* feature: all other classes are (potentially) capable of reaching the status of the "ruling class," in other words, of establishing themselves as the class control-ling the state apparatus:

> What makes the working class into an agency and provides it with a mission is neither its poverty, nor its militant and pseudo-military organization, nor its proximity to the (chiefly industrial) means of production. It is only its structural inabil-

ity to organize itself into yet another ruling class that provides the working class with such a mission. The proletariat is the only (revolutionary) class in history that abolishes itself in the act of abolishing its opposite.

One should draw from this insight the only appropriate conclusion: "dictatorship of the proletariat" is a kind of (necessary) oxymoron, NOT a state form in which the proletariat is the ruling class. We effectively have the "dictatorship of the proletariat" only when the state itself is radically transformed, relying on new forms of the people's participation, which is why there is more than hypocrisy in the fact that, at the highest point of Stalinism when the entire social edifice was shattered by purges, the new constitution proclaimed the end of the "class" character of the Soviet power (voting rights were restored to members of classes previously excluded) and that the Socialist regimes were called "people's democracies"—a sure indication they were not "dictatorships of the proletariat." Where democracy is not enough is with regard to the constitutive excess of representation over the represented.

Democracy presupposes a minimum of alienation: those who exert power can only be held responsible to the people if there is a minimal distance of re-presentation between them and the people. In "totalitarianism," this distance is canceled, the leader is supposed to directly present the will of the people—and the result is, of course, that the (empirical) people are even more radically alienated in their leader: he directly *is* what they "really are," their true identity, their true wishes and interests, as opposed to their confused "empirical" wishes and interests. In contrast to the authoritarian power alienated from its subjects, the people, here the "empirical" people, are alienated *from themselves*.

This, of course, in no way implies a simple plea for democracy and rejection of "totalitarianism": there IS, on the contrary, a moment of truth in "totalitarianism." Hegel already pointed out how political representation does not mean that people already know in advance what they want and then charge their representatives with advocating their interests—they only know it "in itself"; it is their representative who formulates their interests and goals for them, making them "for-itself." The "totalitarian" logic thus makes explicit, posits "as such," a split that always already cuts from within the represented "people."

One should not be afraid here to draw a radical conclusion concerning the figure of the leader: democracy as a rule cannot reach beyond the pragmatic utilitarian inertia, it cannot suspend the logic of "servicing the goods"; consequently, in the same way, there is no self-analysis; since the analytic change can only occur through the transferential relationship to the external figure of the analyst, a leader is necessary to trigger the enthusiasm for a cause, to bring about the radical change in the subjective position of his followers, to "transubstantiate" their identity.

What this means is that the ultimate question of power is not "is it democratically legitimized or not" but *what is the specific character (the "social content") of the "totalitarian excess" that pertains to sovereign power as such, independently of its democratic or nondemocratic character?* It is at this level that the concept of the "dictatorship of the proletariat" functions: in it the "totalitarian excess" of power is on the side of the "part of no-part," not on the side of the hierarchical social order—to put it bluntly, ultimately, they are in power in the full sovereign sense of the term, i.e., it is not only that their representatives temporarily occupy the empty place of power, but, much more radically, they "twist" the very space of state re-presentation in their direction. One can argue that Chavez and Morales are coming close to what could be today's form of the "dictatorship of the proletariat": although interacting with many agents and movements, drawing on their support, his government obviously has a privileged link with the dispossessed of the *favelas*—he is ultimately *their* president, *they* are the hegemonic force behind his rule, and although Chavez still respects the democratic electoral rule, it is clear that his fundamental commitment and source of legitimization is not there, but in the privileged relationship with the dispossessed of the *favelas*. This is the "dictatorship of the proletariat" in the form of "democracy."

A convincing story can be told about the hypocrisy of the Western left, which to a large extent ignores the phenomenal liberal "renaissance" that is going on in Iran's civil society: since the Western intellectual references of this "renaissance" are figures like Habermas, Arendt, and Rorty, even Giddens, not the usual gang of anti-imperialist "radicals," the left makes no fuss when leading figures of this movement lose their jobs and are arrested, etc. With their advocacy of the "boring topics" of division of powers, of democratic legitimization, of the legal defense of human rights, etc., they are viewed with suspicion—they do not appear "anti-imperialist" and anti-American enough. However, one should nonetheless raise the more fundamental question: is bringing Western liberal democracy the true solution for getting rid of the religious-fundamentalist regimes, or are these regimes rather a *symptom* of liberal democracy itself? What to do in cases like that of Algeria or the Palestinian territories, where a "free" democratic election brings "fundamentalists" to power?

When Rosa Luxembourg wrote that "dictatorship consists in the *way in which* democracy is *used* and not in its *abolition*," her point was not that democracy is an empty frame that can be used by different political agents (Hitler also came to power through—more or less— free democratic elections), but that there is a "class bias" inscribed into this very empty (procedural) frame. That is why when radical leftists came to power through elections, their *signe de reconnaissance* is that they move to "change the rules," to transform not only electoral and other state mechanisms but also the entire logic of the political space (relying directly on the power of the mobilized movements; imposing different forms of local self-organization; etc.) to guarantee the hegemony of their base, they are guided by the right intuition about the "class bias" of the democratic form.

NOTES

1. The Democratic Emblem

1. The corresponding passage will be found in *The Republic* book 8, 561d. The version supplied here is from the complete hypertranslation of *The Republic* into French on which I am presently engaged, for publication at the end of 2010. Its aim is to show that Plato is one of our foremost contemporaries. This passage in my translation is taken from chapter 7, "Critique of the Four Precommunist Politics." I naturally dispense with the division of *The Republic* into ten books, an irrelevant piece of textual fiddling perpetrated long after Plato by one or several Alexandrian grammarians.

2. Permanent Scandal

1. *New York Daily Tribune*, June 25, 1853.
2. See Enzo Traverso, *Le Totalitarisme: Le XXe siècle en debat* (Paris: Seuil, 2001).

3. Leon Trotski, *Staline* (Paris: Grasset, 1948).

4. Jacques Rancière, *La Haine de la Democratie* (Paris: La Fabrique, 2005), p. 44. English translation: *Hatred of Democracy*, trans. Steve Corcoran (New York: Verso, 2006).

5. Pierre Rosanvallon, *La légitimité démocratique* (Paris: Seuil, 2008), p. 317. See also Emmanuel Todd, *Après la démocratie* (Paris: Gallimard, 2008). Nicholas Sarkozy was elected president of the French Republic in May 2007. For Todd, Sarkozy is not the real problem, only the symptom of a "general wobbliness of democracy" resulting from the "disappearance of a powerful and stable shared belief system, religious in origin and anchored in localities." As opposed to the empty space postulated by Lefort, Todd thinks that democracy is not viable in the absence of roots and traditions, and that it needs to be rooted once more, even at the risk of arousing identitarian mythologies, national or cultural. One asks: where, in a world of borderless financial flows and fiscal paradises, would you like democracy to be "rooted," M. Todd? And how do you keep this quest for origins and roots from degenerating into a cult of blood and ancestry?

6. Raymond Aron, *Introduction à la philosophie politique: Démocratie et Révolution* (Paris: Livre de Poche, 1997), p. 36.

7. Miguel Abensour, *La Démocratie contre l'État* (Paris: PUF, 1997).

8. Carl Schmitt, *Parlementarisme et démocratie* (Paris: Seuil, 1988).

9. Alain Badiou, *De quoi Sarkozy est-il le nom?* (Paris: Lignes, 2007), p. 42.

10. Badiou, *De quoi Sarkozy*, p. 122.

11. Alain Badiou, "May 68 puissance 4," in *À Babord*, April 2008.

12. Badiou, *De quoi Sarkozy*, p. 134.

13. See Luciano Canfora, *La Démocratie: Histoire d'une idéologie* (Paris: Seuil, 2007).

14. Rancière, *La Haine de la Democratie*, pp. 103–105.

15. Jacques Rancière, *Au bord du politique* (Paris: La Fabrique, 1998), p. 13.

16. *La Philosophie déplacée, Colloque de Cerisy* (Paris: Horlieu, 2006).

17. Cited in Daniel Bensaïd, ed., *Politiquement incorrects: Entretiens pour le XXIe siècle* (Paris: Textuel, 2008).

18. Agnès Heller and Ferencz Feher, *Marxisme et démocratie* (Paris: Maspero, 1981), pp. 127, 237, 301.

19. See Isabelle Garo, *L'Idéologie ou la pensée embarquée* (Paris: La Fabrique, 2009).

20. Jean-Jacques Rousseau, *Le Contrat social* (Paris: Aubier, 1943), p. 187.

21. Louis de Saint-Just, "Institutions républicaines," in *Oeuvres complètes* (Paris: Gallimard, 2004), p. 1087.

22. Ibid., p. 1091.

23. Cornelius Castoriadis, *L'Institution imaginaire de la societé* (Paris: Seuil, 1999), p. 161.

24. Ibid., p. 319.

25. Claude Lefort, *Le Temps présent* (Paris: Belin, 2007), p. 635.

26. Walter Lippmann, *Le Fantôme du public* (Paris: Demopolis, 2008), p. 39.

27. Ibid., p. 143.

28. Rancière, *La Haine de la Démocratie*, p. 60.

29. Lefort, *Le Temps présent*, p. 478.

30. Alexandra Kollontaï, *L'Opposition ouvrière* (Paris: Seuil, 1974), p. 50.

31. See Oskar Anweilher, Serge Bricianer, and Pierre Broué, *Les Soviets en Russie 1905–1921* (Paris: Gallimard, 1972).

32. See Canfora, *La Démocratie*.

33. Rancière, *La Haine de la Democratie*, p. 57.

34. Jacques Rancière, *Le Philsophe et ses pauvres* (Paris: Champs-Flammarion, 2006), p. 204.

35. Lefort, *Le Temps présent*, p. 941.

36. Pierre Bourdieu, *Propos sur le champ politique* (Lyon: Presses Universitaires de Lyons, 2000), p. 71.

37. Simone Weil, *Note sur la suppression générale des partis politiques*, preface by André Breton (Paris: Climats, 2006). First published by Éditions de la table ronde in 1950, seven months after the author's death.

38. Ibid., p. 35.

39. Ibid., p. 61. In his preface, André Breton tries to attenuate this statement by replacing "suppression" with "banishment" (*mise au ban*). This he depicts not as an immediate legislative act but as a historic process,

the outcome of "a long enterprise of collective disillusionment" just as protracted as the hypothetical withering away of the State, politics, and law. But what to do in the meantime?

40. Ibid., p. 65.

41. Karl Marx, *Sur la question juive* (Paris: La Fabrique, 2006), p. 44.

3. "We Are All Democrats Now..."

1. Great brands, Patrick Ruffini reminds us, "evoke feelings that have virtually zero connection to product attributes and specifications." This is as true of Nike and BMW as it was of Obama during the most recent U.S. election, http://www.patrickruffini.com, February 13, 2008.

2. There is no work on this subject superior to Sheldon S. Wolin's *Democracy Inc.* (Princeton: Princeton University Press, 2008).

3. For a more extended account of the deep de-democratizing effects of neoliberal rationality, see my *Les Habits neufs de la politique: Neoliberalisme et neoconservatisme*, introduction by Laurent Jeanpierre (Paris: Les Prairies Ordinaires, 2007).

4. See Michel Foucault on governmentalization of the state in *"Society Must Be Defended": Lectures at the College de France, 1975–76*, trans. D. Macey (New York: St. Martin's, 2003).

5. This expansion is, in part, the issue of well-meaning activists who spy prospects for "winning" in the courts even though democracy may be an inadvertent casualty of their success.

6. See Gordon Silverstein, *Law's Allure: How Law Shapes, Constrains, Saves and Kills Politics* (New York: Cambridge University Press, 2009) and "Law as Politics/Politics as Law," a dissertation in progress by Jack Jackson, Political Science Department, University of California, Berkeley.

7. See my "Porous Sovereignty, Walled Democracy," forthcoming in *La Revue internationale des livres et des idées*.

8. Indeed, this is the premise that even Hobbes struggles to gratify in his fabulous semantic ruses with authors, authorship, and authority, through which he manages to make us author the absolutism of the state which dominates us.

9. Sheldon Wolin formulates this matter a little differently, arguing that only what he calls "fugitive democracy" is possible, episodic expressions by the people of their rightful title. See the final chapters of both *Politics and Vision*, expanded ed. (Princeton: Princeton University Press, 2004) and *Democracy, Inc.* for Wolin's development of this notion.

10. For fuller development of this point, see my "Sovereign Hesitations," in Pheng Cheah and Suzanne Guerlac, eds., *Derrida and the Time of the Political* (Durham: Duke University Press, 2008), and "The Return of the Repressed: Sovereignty, Capital, Theology" in David Campbell and Morton Schoolman, eds., *The New Pluralism: William Connolly and the Contemporary Global Condition* (Durham: Duke University Press, 2008).

11. For a fuller discussion of post-Marxist philosophers pursuing the possibility of resubordinating the economic to a democratic political sphere, see my "The Return of the Repressed."

12. Herbert Marcuse, *One Dimensional Man* (New York: Beacon, 1964).

5. Democracies Against Democracy

1. Jacques Rancière, *La haine de la démocratie* (Paris: La Fabrique, 2005); English translation: *Hatred of Democracy*, trans. Steve Corcoran (New York: Verso, 2006).

2. Jacques Rancière, *La mésentente: Politique et philosophie* (Paris: Galilée, 1995); English translation: *Disagreement: Politics and Philosophy*, trans. Julie Rose (Minneapolis: University of Minnesota Press, 1999).

6. Democracy for Sale

1. Auguste Blanqui, letter to Maillard, June 6, 1852, in *Maintenant, il faut des armes* (Paris: La Fabrique, 2006), pp. 172–186. Translations from the French, unless otherwise noted, are my own; translations of Rimbaud are taken from Paul Schmidt's *Arthur Rimbaud: Complete Works* (New York: Harper and Row, 1976) and have been in some cases slightly modified.

2. Valéry Giscard d'Estaing blog, October 26, 2007.

3. Interview, *RTL*, June 9, 2008.

4. *Le Monde*, June 7, 2008.

5. As reported by the *Canard Enchaîné* and quoted in the *Irish Times,* June 20, 2008.

6. Bosco, Bantry County Cork Eire, http://my.telegraph.co.uk.

7. *France Inter,* June 24, 2008.

8. *Institutions,* June 13, 2008.

9. *Irish Times,* June 14, 2008.

10. *Deutsche Welle,* June 15, 2008.

11. Cited in Dominique Guillemin and Laurent Daure, "L'Introuvable souveraineté de l'Union européene," *L'Action Républicaine,* July 3, 2008, http://action-republicaine.over-blog.com/archive-07-3-2008.html.

12. See Frédéric Bas, "La 'majorité silencieuse' ou la bataille de l'opinion en mai-juin 1968," in P. Artières and M. Zancarini-Fournel, eds., *68: Une histoire collective* (Paris: Découverte, 2008), pp. 359–366.

13. See Sheldon Wolin, "Fugitive Democracy," in *Constellations* 1 (1994): 11–25.

14. See Jacques Rancière, *The Ignorant Schoolmaster,* trans. Kristin Ross (Stanford: Stanford University Press, 1991; see also Josiah Ober, "The Original Meaning of 'Democracy': Capacity to Do Things, Not Majority Rule," *Constellations* 15 (2008): 1–9.

15. Immanuel Wallerstein, "Democracy, Capitalism and Transformation," lecture at Documenta 11, Vienna, March 16, 2001.

16. See Jean Dubois, *Le Vocabulaire politique et social en France de 1869 à 1872* (Paris: Larousse, 1962).

17. See Kristin Ross, *The Emergence of Social Space: Rimbaud and the Paris Commune* (Minneapolis:University of Minnesota Press, 1988; rpt. Verso, 2008); see also Fredric Jameson, "Rimbaud and the Spatial Text," in Tak-Wai Wong and M. A. Abbas, eds., *Rewriting Literary History* (Hong Kong: Hong Kong University Press, 1984).

18. Maxime Vuillaume, *Mes Cahiers rouges au temps de la commune* (Arles: Actes Sud, 1998), pp. 68–69.

19. Luciano Canfora, *Democracy in Europe* (Malden, MA: Blackwell, 2006), p. 120.

20. Rimbaud, cited by Ernest Delahaye in Arthur Rimbaud, *Oeuvres complètes,* ed. Rolland de Renéville et Jules Mouquet (Paris: Gallimard, 1965), p. 745.

21. Harry Truman, January 20, 1949: "We must embark on a bold new program for making the benefits of our scientific advances and industrial progress available for the improvement and growth of underdeveloped areas."

22. See Canfora, *Democracy in Europe,* pp. 214–252.

AUTHORS

GIORGIO AGAMBEN teaches philosophy at the University of Venice. His most recent book is *Le Règne et la gloire* (Seuil, 2008).

ALAIN BADIOU teaches philosophy at the École Normale Supérieure (Rue d'Ulm, Paris). His most recent book is *Second manifeste pour la philosophie* (Fayard, 2008).

DANIEL BENSAÏD teaches philosophy at the University of Paris VIII Saint-Denis. His most recent book is *Marx, mode d'emploi* (La Découverte, 2009).

WENDY BROWN is professor of political science at the University of California at Berkeley. In France she recently published *Les Habits neufs de la politique mondiale* (Les Prairies ordinaires, 2007).

JEAN-LUC NANCY is professor emeritus of the University of Strasbourg. His most recent book is *Verité de la démocratie* (Galilée, 2008).

JACQUES RANCIÈRE is professor emeritus of the University of Paris VIII Saint-Denis. His most recent book is *Le Spectateur émancipé* (La Fabrique, 2008).

KRISTIN ROSS is professor of comparative literature at New York University. Her books in French include *Mai 68 et ses vies ultérieures* (Complexe, 2005) and *Rouler plus vite, laver plus blanc* (Flammarion, 2006). Her forthcoming book is *Rimbaud et la commune* (Textuel).

SLAVOJ ŽIŽEK, a Slovenian philosopher and psychoanalyst, is a guest professor in the department of psychoanalysis of the University of Paris VIII Saint-Denis. He also teaches at Columbia University and Princeton. His most recent book in French is *Le Parallaxe* (Fayard, 2008).